It Takes Balls…

Desmond Flanagan

07711 - 651706

ISBN: 9798682767144

Published by Babysteps Publishing Limited

CONTENTS

ACKNOWLEDGMENTS

I want to dedicate this book to my family, Edel, Anna, Keelan, and Cormac. To those that helped to shape my life, especially Seamus Harkin and the generation that went before me, namely my mum and dad and all their relatives. Special mention must go to Seamus Mallon and all those that shaped the peace process. However, this book would never have been completed without the work of my youngest son Cormac and my table tennis buddy Anthony White.

Prologue

When I asked my son Cormac to take his fancy new camera and video me playing table tennis against the robot he of course glumly responded with, "Let me guess, you want me to then upload the video to the Omagh Table Tennis Facebook page. Can you not just do that yourself? Or will you get it confused with your personal Facebook page as usual?"

"And tell me," he continued, "how come ninety percent of all of the promotional material for the club has your face plastered across it." Upon finishing his sarcastic tirade, the 17-year-old commented on the current state of the room we stood in. The room in question was the third story of the Offices of Des Flanagan Investment Solutions, 9, James Street Omagh, the greatest Financial Advisor on James Street... owned by me of course. The evening sun was piercing through the single pane mid 70's windows of the room that I had recently renovated to include a table tennis table that didn't fit, an automatic table tennis robot that I didn't know how to use and a mini fridge containing four out of date pre-Brexit beers that Cormac was keenly eyeing up.

I had only noticed the dire state of the mini-fridge recently when pointed out by one of my two right-hand men, the Omagh man Phil McCusker when I almost broke the two-meter lockdown rules by inviting him for a beer and a chat. We'll get back to the second right-hand man from Killarney Paul Murphy later. God help you all.

Among a shelf of countless novels and biographies that was directly above the fridge, sat sixteen table tennis trophies, four golf trophies, seven football and Gaelic programs, a coloured print of Parkhead in Glasgow, and two photos of the late great Seamus Harkin, former table tennis coach to Des Flanagan. I was admiring my pride and joy, three programs from when I played international schoolboy table tennis for Ireland between 1979 and 1981 when it hit me. It had been 40 long years since my international heyday.

Junior asked me what all the books were about while keeping one eye on the beers. "The Croatian Civil War, the Irish War of Independence, World War Two books and a host of sports autobiographies," responded Flan the Man, the nickname I had graciously given myself much to the dismay of all those around me. Regarding the biographies, "some of them are fantastic, a couple are good, two are readable and the rest are absolute rubbish. A complete waste of time for both them and especially the reader."

Cormac urged me on somehow holding one of the four beers in his hand. I think he may have known what he was getting himself into. "Paul Kimmage's 'Engage' and 'Rough Ride' alongside 'The Pursuit of Perfection' by Donal McAnallen are the best. 'A Parish far from Home' by Phillip O Connor and 'Mugsy' by Owen Mulligan are good. You can guess about the rest. I don't see how someone can write or even ghost-write three hundred and twenty pages of absolutely nothing." Utter uselessness and more terms that could just have easily been attributed to me as the books flooded my head.

Cormac butted in again, I think you can see a trend here, noting how my OCD must have been kicking in. I got defensive.

"You have all the soccer books together, all the cycling books together, all the Gaelic books beside the rugby ones and you've even kindly given the political and historical books their own little shelf. So, tell me, why aren't there any table tennis books up there?"

With that small question, Cormac had walked out of the room and opened Pandora's box.

"Hi tube," started Bad Des, the perpetual creator of bad ideas and regretful decisions that lives in my head. *"Why don't you write one? You're always giving out about everything and everybody, telling the world how good you are,"* continued the little voice. *"You might be able to start one or talk about one, but*

like your Father, you'll never get around to actually writing one."

"Keep him out of this," I barked back. "I will write a table tennis book about trying to get back into the International arena after a forty-year break. A book about old men playing table tennis. Doesn't that just have Irish sports book bestseller written all over it?"

"Will it be truthful, warts, and all Da?" Junior asked, returning to the room.

"It might be warts and only warts but I will not hold back, fire from the hip son. A 'tell-all' table tennis blockbuster."

He asked me what I will do when it's all finished and written. As Paul Kimmage is the king of this stuff, I will send it down to him to edit it and publish it and we can retire happily ever after. And well, if he thinks it is rubbish, I will self-publish it. Going door to door reckoning back to the old days of being a salesman before taking the financial adviser title. If it is truly rubbish then it will simply find its way to the shelf above the fridge of four beers, strike that, three beers, where all the other rubbish ones sit.

I was sitting in the car half an hour later taking in the quiet desolate country roads when I screamed out loud, "Balls, balls and more balls." I had yet again let my inner demon get the better of me, this ceaseless guy had been part of my life ever since I had met Phil McCusker at the age of 11. I had identified that part of my brain in the book 'The Chimp Paradox' by Professor Steve Peters. It just comes out and needs to be controlled, something which I have frequently failed to do throughout my life.

Once again it was leading me somewhere I didn't want to return to, my past. I refer to it as Bad Des as he had reigned rampant through my teenage years and my table tennis career. Now I'm facing the biggest test of my life, writing a book about table tennis of all things. Fuck you Bad Des.

"Dessie is a waster, Dessie is a waster. He talks all day and does fuck all just like George Cadette," Bad Des droned on.

I'll show you.

It Takes Balls…

1 Irish Classification 17/8/19

Finally, finally, the road back to the international arena starts this morning with the first of seven qualifying tournaments. This morning it's off to Dublin we go. Meet Paul Gallagher or as I call him, 'the Donegal slapper' (I can already hear him piping up "It's called a high precision loop kill"). I've kindly volunteered Paul to drive both Derry head Sean McAnaney and myself the whole way. With him driving it means going through the tight passage at 9 James Street which Paul hates. Spatial awareness is not his greatest strength. Great, he will be stressed from the start. Although these two rivals have become great mates since I returned from the wilderness five years ago, three hours of torture from me on the way down via my nonstop rantings and stupid stories should leave them wrecked and me in prime position for the season. Last year's rankings determine the seedings for today and today's performance will lead to the seeding for the second tournament etc. In simple terms today is absolutely vital for the year ahead and my long-overdue return to international table tennis, thus putting Bad Des in his place once and for all. Who would ever miss it?

Process, process, process Des. Follow what the books say. Table tennis bag first. Well in my case it is actually a golf hold-all that I won five years ago. In fact, the last thing that I won before telling everyone that I was on the way to being a single figure handicapper. That didn't really work out either, sixteen is not quite the same. Stop, stop, stop, back to the process. Bag. From the bottom up Des. Three pairs of socks, new table tennis shoes with 'go fast' strips down the side, spare pair of shoes, two pairs of shorts, three shirts to make me look fit (fuck off Bad Des I am not listening to you), tracksuit, two hand towels, two bats (unlike 10 bat McAlister from Cookstown) and finally food and water bottles. Great, great start Des. What about the gun jokes Des? No need, my forehand, which I call "the big dog", is my weapon of mass destruction today.

Let's go. Here we go, here we go, here we go, here we go. Louder Des, louder.

"Wake up Des, wake up Des, are you dreaming again? Are the nightmares back?" my wife Edel shouted. "What is going on? It must be the jetlag," she continued.

"Where am I?" I asked, startled.

Edel explained to me that we were in Hell's Kitchen, New York for the holiday that I had promised the family when I booked it last month around the 12th of July after giving out about something, who knows what.

"Up you get. We've got a busy day ahead. The kids are so excited about seven days in the Big Apple. Here we go, here we go." to which I responded "Any chance of a cup of tea first? Also, could you tell me what date it is?"

"Certainly Desmond, it is the 17th day of August 2019. Come on get up. Keelan has that information you asked for after wrecking the in-house laptop trying to work the Wi-Fi, that wasn't like you"

The room I found myself in was flanked by two bare brick-red walls with an open window on the front side adjacent to a loud prehistoric air conditioner. The black-rimmed window stared out at the busy 'Freewheelin Bob Dylan'-esque streets. A brown UPS truck lounged on the footpath, or should I say sidewalk, with both doors missing and a relaxed man hanging out the driver side window, cigarette in hand. Down the road lay 'Down the street', a local bar with a target audience far younger and trendier than myself which I of course would spend many hours in over the next week, both with and without my family.

Although early in the day an air of humidity hung over the city only penetrated by an unforgettable smell of rubbish boiling in the harsh summer heat. We were in New York all right.

"You must be the biggest plonker in the world," my dear friend Bad Des butted in. *"As you readily admit to anyone who will listen, you are the most organised person in the world yet you book the family holiday on the Friday before what? Yes, the day before the start of your journey to where, you big plonker? Yes, international table tennis. Get a grip."*

Before I left the house, I just had to see who all had entered the Irish classification tournament. I was trying to convince myself everything would be alright when 'you know who' decided to pipe up again. *"Forget about the big two Des, here are a few other names that you will struggle with; McAlister, Shaw, Pemberton, Gibbons, Pender, Burke, Norgrove, Lappin, Butler, Looney, Nabney, Cunningham, Kareem Samir, Pierre Bouhey, and your so-called friends Gallagher and McAnaney,"* he taunted.

Edel stormed back into the room to accuse me of falling asleep again. Maybe the shouts and curses at Bad Des were said a bit too loudly. *"Also, I forgot to mention the men with the great Irish names. Who? Branislav Jakovetic, Nebojsa Fabric and Pawel Sulkowski. Ireland is a changing place with plenty of players you never considered you waster."*

Bad Des continued his tirade. *"Finally, just to wreck your holidays completely I will mention one last name."*

"Who for fucks sake?" I almost screamed.

"Your old buddy Brian Finn."

Jesus, that was the final straw. Brian f..ing Finn. If that man was not pulling me for foul serves (guilty), taking towel breaks ("only after every 12 points Mr. Flanagan" I can hear him droning on), he was actually beating me. Where the hell did I put that gun?

"Fuck off Bad Des," I pleaded, totally beaten. "Will you at least leave me alone for seven days to enjoy my holidays?" I gingerly asked.

"Agreed but two final names. John Fall and Brian Orr." Surprisingly, I smiled, which annoyed Bad Des. Your telling me Brian Orr still moves?

I found myself uttering the name of Brian Finn under my breath as I trudged through the creaking sliding glass door of our Air B&B, wait never mind, Air B&B's are illegal in New York. I found myself uttering the name Brian Finn under my breath as I trudged through the sliding glass door of our perfectly legal apartment on lease to us for '6 months', past my jetlagged daughter who had collapsed on the sofa unlikely to recover until at least halfway through the holiday as per usual. Past my aforementioned son Cormac and straight into the arms of my 18-year-old 6 foot 3 rugby player, bodybuilder, academic, and ever caring eldest son Keelan, who had the notion that I was about to buy him the first beer of the holiday. No clue where he got that idea from.

Keelan had been researching pubs across New York ever since the holiday was announced. Maybe as a coping method to stay sane for an entire week with the family, away from his friends and the gym. We were yet to tell him about the licensing laws as we didn't want to completely break the poor lad.

"Blue Finn, Finn MAC Cools, and finally Finn's Corner" he shouted loudly. "Finn's corner is in Brooklyn Da. You always go on and on and on about walking over the Brooklyn Bridge and going for a few beers."

My eldest son tackled me in a big Russian bear hug, mistaking the tears falling down my face for tears of joy. How was he to know the effect that the simple mention of the word Finn would have on me?

God help me.

It Takes Balls…

2 New York

Maybe it wasn't such a bad thing that I missed the first tournament. Despite spending most of the week being dragged around Manhattan by Keelan in his search for a MAGA hat, it turned out to be one of the best family holidays I've ever been on. We hit all the major tourist hotspots from the Statue of Liberty to the Wall Street Bull, but the most memorable moments came from time spent with the family. Anna and Edel were overjoyed when we got tickets to see the brilliant 'Rock of Ages' musical and Cormac couldn't have been happier, spending hours in the two-story guitar superstore at Times Square, which was just two blocks from our accommodation.

The Thursday night in New York was spent at a quaint steakhouse just around the corner. I had regrettably told Keelan that he could order the most expensive steak on the menu. I'll never forget the look on his face when half a cow came out on a countertop sized slate, the thing was twice the size of the lad's head, which is really saying something. That night me and the two boys agreed to go down to Chinatown the next day in search of a cheap knockoff watch for Keelan's school formal, followed by lunch in Little Italy.

By 2 o'clock the next day the sun was out, and I was having an Italian beer with my lunchtime pizza alongside my two sons. The everyday pressures of working within the financial services industry, looking after the pensions and investments of over 500 people, now belonged to a different world. The holiday had been brilliant, and I was now participating in my favourite pastime, daydreaming. During this time, me and my little friend Bad Des frequently indulge in a bit of sparring. In my early teens, I had retired from boxing after three fights with a one hundred percent record to concentrate on my soon to be international table tennis career.

Looking at my teenage sons made me reflect on my own teenage years and how things had changed for the better. In the years between 1979 and 1981 when I had been 16 and 18 respectively, just over 311 people had been killed in The Troubles. This fact had always alarmed me and looking at my own boys I was grateful that normality was nearly upon us. (By the way, I had lost those 3 fights, thus the 100% record and the switch to the safer game of table tennis.)

I will forever be grateful for the fact that my job as a financial advisor has allowed me to access hundreds of families from traditionally unionist backgrounds. Some were Unionists with a big U and some were just unionists. My last training course in October 1992 had specifically warned us not to ever touch two topics, namely religion, and politics, or was it politics and religion? Just like my big lump of an eldest lad, I was never the greatest at taking instruction. My very first client meeting took place outside of the village of Newtownstewart, County Tyrone. The surname of the man I was visiting gave the game away before it had even started.

We were on opposite sides. I stated thus "I am going to name two subjects and Billy you are going to decide the order."

I immediately detected a smile and knew instantly that my career in financial services would never be boring. "Politics and Religion," I stated

Billy instantly opted for the safer of the two, religion. "You start Des"

"Well I am a bad Catholic, and by that, I mean a Catholic that knows little about Catholicism rather than just being a bad Catholic."

"I am a level below that regarding being a prod," Billy replied. "But I know a few tunes that you might be interested in," he smiled.

About four hours later I emerged into the darkness with a stupid grin on my face, having signed up my first unionist as a client, although I knew virtually nothing about what I had just sold him. The buzz was incredible, and his stories were even dafter than mine. The common denominator between us had been our love for football. Billy, of course, had not been told of my love of Glasgow Celtic F.C. especially as he had a large poster of the four in a row winning Rangers squad on his wall alongside some other stuff only seen in the away end at Celtic F.C. Unfortunately, Billy's team were on a nine in a row run which he kindly pointed out on my return visits. In the years to come a pattern had developed, five minutes business, two hours football - Great stuff - I loved the big fool and still visit him annually but his tune is now different as the tables have been turned regarding Scottish football.

Billy had also asked if I had ever done any big away trips and he was not talking about Glentoran or Ballymena United but Europe. I sidestepped him for a few years but later I told him the following story which was to be very influential for the rest of my life.

In 1981, March to be specific, myself, Stevie Rice, and Mr. Phillip McCusker set out on an epic trip to Brussels to watch the Republic of Ireland attempt to qualify for the 1982 World Cup finals to be held in Spain. We had the best team we had ever had but unfortunately it was Billy's lot that were to qualify, and memories of Gerry Armstrong's famous goal are now part of the history of this part of the world. Billy from Newtownstewart and Billy Bingham's crew. A lot of Billies where I am from including my brother-in-law Billy Allen. His story will have to wait.

McCusker was centre stage here, he had been at Lansdowne Rd for the 3-2 victory over Cyprus and the 2-1 victory over Holland. He convinced me to take a break from table tennis and head to see us stuff Belgium. Jan f…king Cueleman's Belgium. 15th of October 1980 to be precise (still have the ticket). In the first leg, Albert Claytens scored early for Belgium but Grealish replied for the fighting Irish on the 42-minute mark. If we could only finish the job in the second half, we would nearly be there. Chance after chance went a-begging. So tense, so tense and exhilarating but the game finished 1-1.

Instantly McCusker screams, "We will finish them bastards in Brussels"

Putting his hand out he declared, "Shake on it Flanagan, we will go." 'Be careful when you shake Phil's hand' is now in the lexicon.

Somehow, we convinced our Fathers and Mothers and convinced Phil's near neighbour Stevie Rice to join us. Stevie was easily convinced as he was now working as a trainee barman in MJ O'Kanes's bar at the top of High Street and had money in his pocket, something that me and Phil needed access to. Shoestring would be pushing it to describe the budget we had gathered. The match was scheduled to be played exactly 6 weeks before our A levels, the exams that would shape our lives. Balls, balls, and more balls to that. Imagine Keelan asking Edel for permission to take a 735-mile bus journey before his A levels. It would be a stupid 18-year-old that would ask. But we were undoubtedly stupid 18-year-olds, even on a good day.

The trip was painstakingly organised by Mr. McCusker. Pain being the appropriate word as we had to hitchhike down and up to the offices of Magic Bus Dublin to get the bus tickets. No Idea how Phil convinced the FAI (Football Association of Ireland) to give 3 kids from the North tickets.

Belgique – Rep. Irlande
Belgie – IERSE

"Phil, why are the tickets in two languages?" I asked quite innocently.

"I thought history, politics and current affairs were your department Desmond." I was beginning to detect a tone and I wasn't happy with the use of the term 'Desmond' when my name is clearly Des, Dessy, or Dessie. Obviously.

"Flemish Desmond. The southern part of Belgium speaks Flemish and want to break away from the rest of the country."

"Just like the Freestaters did in 1921," I taunted back and ran off.

The above conversation took place in a wee bar beside the Busáras bus station in Dublin. The trick is to always have a bit of knowledge that no one else had. Finding that against Phil is never easy.

"As the son of my former employer would Mr. Flanagan junior like a pint of Guinness? Phil, I have already ordered us two." Stevie asked.

By now Phil and I had declared peace but the mention

of Da had instantly brought a smile to Phil's face as we both knew where this was heading.

"Stevie, tell us about when you were stopped by the British Army and Dessie senior told them to arrest you."

Stevie replied, "I have no idea what I was doing but I remember the usual nonsense, too many stupid questions, and too many particularly stupid answers but 'what is your current employment?' was the final straw."

"Trainee maggot breeder? Son, I will ask you one final time."

Stevie had responded to the RUC officer with "I am not your son thank fuck." The RUC had been called after the British Army had got nowhere with Mr. Rice.

"Stop, stop, what is the problem here?" asked the RUC commander. Five minutes later Mr. Rice was back at the start of his story, a common theme back in the '70s and 80's

"Mr. Rice, you are telling me that you are a trainee maggot breeder employed by a mister Desmond Flanagan Senior from Omagh." A couple of younger policemen had gathered round. If there was a sweep in the station on a weekly basis for the most ridiculous response to a question, Stevie may have been the provider of the overall winner.

"If you idiots are going to arrest me for giving a factually correct answer I want to talk to my solicitor," Stevie continued. "If you do not believe me why do you not ask him?" He was pointing to the SS Moore sports shop opposite the City Hall. Marched into the shop, Stevie demanded to talk to the owner. Five minutes later Stevie had the owner explaining who Des Flanagan senior from Omagh was. A stupid grin had appeared on the owner's face. He disappeared for a minute and returned with a small box. Mr. Flanagan supplies this shop with the finest maggots for course fishing, lifting one and popping it in his mouth. A small percentage of course anglers still do this today as their party piece.

"Before we let you go, Mr. Rice, we need to confirm this information."

At Flanagan's Baby Corner and Fishing Tackle Emporium on Sedan Avenue Omagh, opposite the showgrounds home of Omagh Town F.C, stood the aforementioned Mr. Flanagan senior, holding the shop's landline. "Balls" was his answer when asked if he was the employer of a certain Mr. Rice.

"Who? Nobody by that name has ever done a full day's work for me," my father truthfully informed the now totally confused officer (Stevie worked part-time three days a week in one of those government schemes to give taigs a job). "Arrest him, he is bloody useless."

This went on for about 10 minutes until the owner of the sports shop took the phone out of the officer's hand and said hello to Des senior. For a further 10 minutes, the policeman heard nothing but laughter as Dessie told one tall tale after another. Realising he was being stitched up the officer released Mr. Rice.

Back in Dublin Stevie asked me, "Why don't you tell your stupid maggot story and your attack on the British army?" he laughed.

Two things the British Army did not like about the land of many names were terrorists (for obvious reasons) and smart arses. Fortunately, I fell into the latter camp.

Over the next half an hour I recalled my one and only direct action against the might of the British Army. On a bitterly cold January with snow falling, a notion entered my head. (Once a notion enters the head of the male species it is virtually impossible to get it out.) My bedroom shared with 'big brother' Seamus, six years older, overlooks the length of Sedan Avenue with a view over the home of the legendary

Omagh Town F.C. I was able to watch as the army trucks left from their St Lucia barracks which stood at the start of the Derry Road. It takes two minutes for them to pass by Neilly and Cowan's, a petrol station beside the house and employer of Billy Allen, my sisters' future husband.

With my weapon prepared and plan hatched I returned to my lookout post. The time was 8 pm, this was vital as it needed to be dark so from the lights I could determine if the trucks were coming my way. Once they turned left the operation was a 'go'.

Shit, the second Saracen's door was only slightly open, I forgot that it had been snowing, they must have been sheltering from the cold. Here we go, here we go. My projectile of snow with its precious cargo was launched, hitting three inches too far to the left, but close enough to hear "what the fuck." About 30% of the cargo landed inside the truck and I could see two big ugly soldiers jumping out shouting.

"Get them off me, get them off me now!"

The soldier looking my way had worked it out, I was just standing there admiring my shot instead of moving into position (as far away as possible), a problem that would follow me into my table tennis career when I have launched the 'Big Dog'.

The chase was on. Although I was not the quickest, this was my home venue. I was off behind the service station and over the wall down to the river. Immediate right, turning back on myself (a dangerous military manoeuvre) heading along the 'traditional route' me and Phil take to get into Omagh Town matches without paying. Another wall jumped and I was standing just to the left of the centre circle of the showgrounds, somewhere I had always dreamed of being but lacking pace and having two left feet meant a second sports career ended before it had even started. From here I could see what was happening through the cracks in the two turnstiles straight opposite Mum and Dad's shop. My mum ran the Baby Corner and my father ran the fishing tackle shop, actually Bridget did, the good-looking girl that Seamus hadn't and would never have the bottle to ask out. I swore that I would never let myself make the same mistake.

I needed a story just in case and thankfully me and Phil had a stash of footballs close to the pitch. Football now stashed up my jumper I stared through the turnstile again to see the kerfuffle breaking out. Two soldiers and one slightly annoyed Des Flanagan senior were having a heated conversation, debate, or something to that effect. The RUC were next to arrive. The army was always easier to deal with as you just had to talk about football and deflect attention from whatever they were asking you. Over the next 20 minutes, I watched many hands gesturing and pointing of fingers all whilst I was getting my balls frozen off. I really had not planned this well. Snowball equals snow, snow equals cold, cold equals frozen... obviously, Da, Da, Super Da was not letting anybody in part because a Cream of the Barley awaited him, and he may have been in a mood. You always had to be careful how you framed a question to him. Any possibility of a stupid answer or window for him to jump through to start one of his stories was always taken. I have listened to the master over the years and learned.

I waited another ten minutes hoping my father had not locked the door which he frequently forgot to do. I tried the handle. Open. Thank God! Quickly locking the door, I proceeded through the fishing tackle shop, through the baby corner, turning sharp left up the stairs. At the top of the stairs another sharp left then a second right would have gotten me back to base, a base from which I fully intended to stand down all future military operations due to a one hundred percent success rate and the fact that I had been scared shitless.

"Where the hell are you coming from junior?" shouted Da.

"Table tennis Da."

"It's a Thursday night," he shouted back. St Colmcilles table tennis club operated 7-10 Monday, Wednesday, and Friday nights.

Quick on my toes, I responded, "League match da… of course we won, the mad McGreads from Clanabogan didn't stand a chance."

"Why have you got a football up your jumper then?"

"Football practice da, me and Phil over in the showgrounds."

"At this time of night."

Ignoring the question, I asked "By the way, what were the police here for? Was Seamus out in that yellow Ford Escort again?"

"Don't you mind?" Da was about a foot away from me, I could smell the scent of whiskey hanging in the air. "Were you playing table tennis outside? You look frozen." He grabbed my right hand.

"Those McGreads never put the heating on. But I stuffed them, although Paul gave me a game then folded later on." Folding, later on, is a trait he still has to this day.

"Right, off to bed son… By the way, if that little incident had got in the papers," he paused, "it would have been great for business"

Five minutes later with a hot water bottle held tightly to me, I reviewed what had just been said. Clearly, he knew I had been guilty as sin but why no attack, and good for business? Fucks sake "Army attacked by maggot bomb, police investigating." Every Tom, Dick, and Harry would have been in looking for fishing licences and maggots. This would have had to be a winter strategy. Maggots inside snowballs. I drifted off to dreamland with a big stupid grin on my face, military career over.

Back on the trip to Brussels. The next few days were to be epic as three young fools launched their attack on the mainland. No not that one, Europe. The next problem occurred leaving the shores of England heading to Zeebrugge. Always having to celebrate leaving England we had Stella Artois in hand. With a complete lack of respect for its alcoholic volume, "This is like drinking water" was uttered by one or all of us at one stage or another during the trip.

The magic bus ticket included the ferry to England, the bus to Dover via London, the ferry to Zeebrugge, and a bus to some small train station about 20 kilometres (we were in Europe now) outside Brussels. The problem was that we three lads had changed into full military uniforms, namely various 10-year-old republic of Ireland/Celtic jerseys on the bus before going into the bar. Now pissed, the bus driver was refusing to let us on. Stevie gave him a touch because he was English, and Phil assumed military command. He barked my orders, "Sort this out, Des."

I confidently stepped forward trying to steady myself. Pausing for a few seconds I smiled (I was completely pissed by now) and offered my apologies. I held out my hand and smiled again. I did not utter a word (anyone who knows me knows the odds of this). Finally, I broke the driver and our road to the World Cup finals was back on. I nodded to commander McCusker as he took Stevie under his wing.

86 minutes into the match I was fast asleep. 733 miles of everything bar a plane to watch a match and I am fast asleep. A dig to the side from McCusker. "Four minutes to go and it's off to sunny Spain for us."

Then something that stills sticks in my mind, the reason why I still hate the 87th minute of football matches, dodgy free kicks and I mean check with doctor google level dodgy. Then that wee shit, Jan f…king Ceulemans, pops up and scores.

The final score was a 1-0 defeat, the first of many overseas defeats. We ventured back out of the Heysel stadium that was soon to be infamous for the trampling of Juventus fans by Liverpool supporters in the 1985 European Cup final. Just over four years later, on the night before my last law exam at Liverpool University, I listened to the carnage. Eventually, 39 would die and over 600 were injured. Liverpool F.C and their supporters would rightfully bring up Hillsborough and the slaughter of 96 innocents. In my opinion, Liverpool F.C and their wonderful fans need to revisit Heysel and their part in that disaster.

The three not so merry men retreated back to their hostel and a small bar they had started the day in, right beside the hostel. Phil asked, "Why pass this bar?" Without any sensible retort, I followed him into Bar One. I have since developed a scheme to avoid going into bars that I do not want to go into. It's called 'buyers' choice', vital in Amsterdam but not as vital in either Munich, Stuttgart, or Bilbao as we may see later.

Problem number two. Where the hell was the hostel? What was the name of the bar beside it? Has anybody any money left? Phil was being very, very sheepish but I knew not to ask. From within my sock, I produced the hostel card. Genius, my thinking which I still use today is as follows; If you get mugged, who the hell is going to take off your socks. It's almost foolproof.

1 pm 26/3/81: "I cannot find the tickets."

We were fully packed and looking forward to our 733-mile return trip (not). Hungover, broke and in a total daze, we were quickly awoken to this news from our leader.

"What do you mean you can't find the tickets?" I

demanded.

"I have some good news; we have 10 Belgian francs and the magic bus tickets from London back to Dublin."

"We are in fucking Belgium Phil, what about the tickets from Brussels to London?"

"Where are we?" uttered Stevie emerging from the hostel in a complete daze.

"You tell him, Phil." I marched across the street now agreeing with Phil's theory from the previous day regarding passing bars. Maybe Phil was right after all.

Twenty minutes later after blowing 100% of my remaining budget on a Stella to steady the nerves, we trudged out and along one of those beautiful Boulevards common in many European cities. The two likely lads kept a safe distance from each other and especially myself.

My head was spinning, the ground was moving, A levels just 6 weeks away, it would take 7 weeks to walk home. I spotted something at the corner of my eye (international table tennis players have this ability). "So Phil, you are telling me that we have bus tickets from London to Dublin, how much money do you have in your pockets? Well, I bet you all of it that I can solve the issue." Phil laughed; Stevie hoped.

With that, Des Flanagan changed his life. He confidently stepped out in front of a bus, left hand fully extended RUC-esque, and summoned the poor startled and wrecked bus driver to pull over. Des nodded to the boys, Phil demoted from commander in chief, as a budding international bullshitter went to work. Three minutes later two very tired and one very excited Omagh Town F.C supporters entered the bus. Having lost the match, we were quick to change our allegiance back to our beloved Omagh Town. At this stage in life, the three of us were the full committee for the junior Omagh Town Supporters Club. We headed towards the rear of the bus and parked ourselves four rows from the back. Thirty-two seconds later three cans were passed sweetly into our hands and the greatest journey of my life started, although I didn't realise it yet. Three hours later I was into story forty-seven, the passengers started moving to the back of the bus to join us. Cheap but beautiful Stella cans were flowing. Stevie was singing, Phil was pepping up and Flan the Man was in full swing. Tale after tale, some tall but some not, some with an element of truth but mostly not.

The ferry journey was next, by this stage the passengers had made a collection for the three of us. Phil was dispatched to the bar, fully reaping the benefits of no longer being in charge. Then came the bus journey to London and then finally free overnight accommodation with their leader, a Dubliner who frequented O' Donoghue's in Dublin, and a real storyteller. Welcome to the London Republic of Ireland supporters club. With my international eye, I had spotted people with Republic of Ireland shirts entering the bus and watched carefully as the bus approached, calculating in my head, always waiting until the odds were completely in my favour before I attacked as above.

Leaving for the small matter of a journey from London to Omagh our confidence was restored. The lads laughed the whole way home. We vowed to hunt those London Irish lads down and repay their generosity.

3 1981

We finally arrived back in Omagh from our Brussels trip on Saturday 28/03/81, absolutely wrecked but feeling proud that we had somehow managed to pull off this adventure without major incident. The result of the match was not our fault, we were not the ones playing. There were six weeks to our A levels and we had to repay our parents. "Go if you must but study, study, and only study when you get back." At this point, I only wanted peace and quiet and to make my mother proud. However, circumstances would take over.

On the morning of May the 5th 1981, Bobby Sands died in the Maze prison just outside Belfast and chaos ensued. I was very quickly going to have to pick sides within the nationalist community, a decision that was going to alter the course of my life.

The bus journey in from Lislap to Omagh was tense, to say the least. My dad had recently sold the shop and moved 5 miles out into the wilderness. One wrong comment would have set the bus off. I was extremely nervous because I had a fair inkling of what was likely to happen if I ever made it into school. The bus depot was absolute chaos, there were at least seven or eight fights taking place all over the place. Omagh CBS and St. Pat's Secondary School were the nationalist schools in town, alongside the Loreto Convent for young ladies. A few of the young ladies were actively involved in what I was seeing. Taunting the nationalists were the Omagh Academy boys and girls and the Omagh County Secondary School which provided the bigger numbers. In the middle of this, the RUC and army were trying to keep the peace.

Having just recovered from Brussels, I needed this like a hole in the head. History and current affairs were always my thing. I was studying three A levels: English Literature, History, and Economic History. I would read every book regarding the two world wars, the Korean war, the Vietnam, etc, I was your man. Maybe because I was from a so-called middle-class family and mainly because of my parents, I detested violence and I sensed what was coming next.

"Right lads, the whole class are heading straight over to the academy and we will show those Orange Bastards who is in charge here." Two or three minutes of rowing ensued, then came the call for arms. Balls, balls, balls… decision time.

"Why does it always have to be somebody else's fault?" I asked.

"What the fuck do you mean Flanagan?"

"Why does everything that happens here have to be their fault?"

"I am going nowhere and I'm not fighting a so-called war that I do not believe in." I continued.

Roy McLaughlin, my highly successful table tennis doubles partner, was a Protestant lad and went to the local County Secondary School. For the next couple of minutes, I argued with the lads from a republican background. Eventually, only about three or four of them left for the academy. The bulk of the lads said nothing, scared of the consequences. The lads duly returned later at lunch time to take their revenge on me.

After the final blow was landed, one of them spat the following at me, "Flanagan, you are nothing more than a West Brit." This hurt more than any of their punches. With my 100% boxing record, I knew how to take a punch. That wouldn't be the last time in my life that the 'West Brit' insult would be hurled my way.

Thank God I made that small stand, maybe I was still feeling guilty regarding the maggot bomb attack two years prior.

When the A level results came out in August, I was in tears once again. I now had my escape route out of 'loo loo land', as I was now calling the north. But now they were tears of joy. Phil had also got his escape results and we had repaid our parents' faith in us. "I am heading up to the Dale Des and I'll see you in Bogan's around 12."

I first had to go see my mum who after running the very successful bit of the family business, the Baby Corner, was now employed in Johnson's shop behind the school. The family business had mainly failed due to alcoholism. She was probably the only Catholic employee in Johnson's store at the time, a sad reflection of things in the north at the time.

"An A and two Cs" are the proudest words I have ever uttered to my mum. She repeated them as loudly as possible because I had beaten all the sons and daughters of the other employees. She gave me the biggest hug and somehow a £20 note found its way into my pocket. This money would be wisely invested in Bogans over the next few hours. Little did I know at the time that within four years my beautiful mum would be dead.

That afternoon and evening of results day were some of the most enjoyable hours of my young life. Me and Phil were heading off, me to Aston University in Birmingham and Phil to the Polytechnic in Pontypridd. Not long back from our international travels and now confirmed as 'intelligent', I was back in action as an international bullshitter telling tale after tale about how we took on Brussels and won.

Writing this A level story years later also brings back tears, as the third member of our group that day was a certain Brian 'doe' McGuigan. Sadly 'doe' was taken from us early when he died from an allergic reaction. To this day I drive into Omagh every A level results night to wander around the town, all to remember one man. Brian 'doe' McGuigan, RIP, you are sadly missed.

4 Journey To Leinster Open

Thirty-eight years and two months since my own A level results day and I was frequently popping back to talk to 'Doe' Mc Guigan. My mind seems to operate totally independently from me, and I have little control of how, where, and why it jumps all over the place. I have learned to use this to drift off into my own world and I know that today will be no different. The boys had been in touch during the week to update me on the results from the first tournament. The big two had played each other in the final and Nebojsa Gabric and Kieran Burke had lost in the semi-finals. Paul Gallagher had lost in the quarters along with Phil Shaw, Dave Pender, and Kariem Sabir. No major damage from my point of view but little wriggle room remained. It was time to get organised.

Again, the routine. Three pairs of socks, new table tennis shoes with 'go fast' stripes down the side, spare pair of shoes, two pairs of shorts, three shirts to make me look fit, a tracksuit, two hand towels, two bats and a water pistol just in case Brian Finn annoyed me.

As I live five miles out of Omagh in the traditionally Unionist area known as Dunmullan, I have always enjoyed my little spin in to meet the lads. As the stock market was close to record highs, the stress levels had been lower than normal regarding my work as an independent financial advisor. Apart from running a highly efficient and loving home, Edel is also a partner in the business. She is responsible for writing all the annual financial reports and she also performs the task of office manager. I give the advice and poor Ciaran, my nephew, has to do all the real work or so he says.

Driving off, I was leaving a happy home where Keelan would be trying to get a full team out to play for the Omagh Accies under 18s rugby team and Cormac, or junior as I call him, would be playing with his new toy (another guitar). Our eldest child and the brains of the family, Anna, had already headed back to Glasgow University where she was in the third year of her medicine degree. I, of course, thought Glasgow was a fantastic choice of city as it opened the door for the odd visit to Parkhead (sorry Anna).

As I headed off up by the Orange Hall, with its union jack fluttering in the wind, I was wondering how come things have worked out so well for me. I am married to the woman I love, living in the town I love, and living in a beautiful house in a stunning location. The kids are a great reflection on Edel but still I was unsettled. What exactly the problem was, I was not quite sure, maybe it was the land of many names and what lies ahead for all of us? Like most 56-year olds I have lived through 'The Troubles' and emerged hopefully without too much damage, but I know that it gnaws away at me. We had bought the house and moved into it on the 8th of August 1998. I wanted to buy a house close to the Gortin Glens Forest Park but the house that we eventually settled on was in Dunmullan. I wanted to move forward. If we had kids, I wanted them to grow up with Protestant neighbours, something that I had never done. Before table tennis I had never even properly met a Protestant.

Exactly one week after moving into our home the Omagh Bomb ripped our town and almost our community apart. At that stage, Edel was working as a nurse and I had to drive her home from a wedding in Enniskillen so that she could head into the Omagh County Hospital. It was years later before she opened up about the horrors that she witnessed that day.

A couple of days before that wedding a few of Edel's friends had phoned me looking for reassurance regarding them staying in the north. With the Good Friday Agreement being signed in April 1998, I completely reassured the girls and also stated that "Nothing ever happens in Omagh."

After my meeting with Billy from just outside Newtownstewart, yes, the big Rangers fool, I had vowed to continue the trend of talking politics and religion with all my clients. Over the years I have found this fascinating and I also feel privileged to get this opportunity. Terms like Protestants and unionists have a different meaning to me than they do for most of my nationalist friends. I know them and have started putting myself in their position to see how I would feel if I was a unionist surrounded by nationalists and republicans. To date, my large client bank is made up of sixty percent unionists, thirty-eight percent nationalists, and two percent 'I don't give a running jump.'

Balls, balls, and more balls. Again, I had just been startled back to reality as I passed the apartments on my left where Ronan Kerr was shamefully murdered in April of 2011. A young lad from a traditionally Nationalist background that had joined the PSNI to protect us all, but had lost his life for what reason? "To unite our country."

Balls, balls, and more balls to that. Though the moment of hope that came out of this tragedy was how his coffin was carried by members of the PSNI and the Gaelic football community, this was hope for the future. That beautiful young man had given his life but what have I given? I asked myself. Unfortunately, as you drive through the land of many names there are far too many sites like that one.

"Paul, Sean, how are things?" I shouted to the two lads when I arrived in Omagh, as I clambered into Paul's car.

"You know yourself, Des, how did New York go? Are you ready to take on the world of table tennis again?"

"How did your fitness regime go; did you lose that stone of weight you promised?" the two lads continued.

Before long I realised that I had told the boys so many stories at the end of last season that I had not remembered my end of it, especially the losing weight and getting super fit bit.

"Through the archway Paul, turn left and first right down the hill" I instructed the designated driver, wondering if he was just winding me up by letting on that that he didn't know his way around Omagh.

Paul Gallagher is from Letterkenny and is the Chief Finance Officer for some American company in Donegal (I should probably listen more when Paul answers a question). Also, in the car, in the front passenger seat also known as my preferred seat, was Sean McAnaney from Derry, a town with many names; Derry, Londonderry, second city, Foyleside, etc.) When I ran the marathon in that city in 1982 the medal read 'Foyle Festival Marathon 1982', and when Edel ran it recently it read 'Walled City Marathon'. We really do have an issue regarding names in this 'wee north.'

Down the hill past John Street's McGale's Furniture Shop, home to Omagh's only double ironman. Onto Kevlin Road and up past the Omagh CBS school. Left, right, left, and off we were to Dublin for the second tournament of the season.

"Did I ever tell you the story about me and Phil McCusker getting in trouble?" I enquired.

"No, but I feel like you are about to tell us," Sean piped up with a nod to Paul.

Me and Phil were at the back of the class talking away about Celtic F.C. obviously a little bit too loudly when 'Bungee' Brother O'Shea asked while touching his glasses "When are you going to start working Mr. Flanagan?"

Slightly annoyed that Bungee was directing this question at me instead of McCusker I immediately got my answer ready, realising that it could fall into the smart ass category. "Probably when I leave school, sir," I answered with a smug grin on my face.

Balls, balls, and more balls I thought as Bungee beelined for me. Was he going to hit me on the left or right side of the jaw? Whack, right on the left side and everybody was laughing.

Charlie McGinn and Micky McCann shouted abuse at me, and Bungee balanced everything up with a cheap blow to the right side of my jaw.

"How come I got hit for a technically correct answer?" I demanded at Brother O'Shea, to which he retorted "Shut up Flanagan."

Back in the car to Dublin, Sean stated "That's not very funny" to which Paul said, "he should have hit you harder."

The reason that story had jumped into my head was that Phil McCusker lives just 2 minutes from the school, or three minutes if you walk at Phil's pace.

Now that Paul was driving on the main road to Dublin, I started drifting off. Fortunately, this time it was into one of my favourite lands, that of Seamus Harkin and St Colmcille's Table Tennis Club. The Club was founded in

1975 and operated three nights a week from 7 to 10 pm; Monday, Wednesday, and Friday. How I started I do not know, but I quickly became top dog (in my head at least). I lived for those nights; I was running away from the verbals at home which always started after the fourth Cream of the Barley Whiskey. From this base, we launched ourselves onto the Ulster Table Tennis scene. Tournaments started to be won and selection for the under 14 and under 17 Ulster teams came along. Table tennis in Ulster was mainly played by protestants out of church halls and sometimes orange halls. The YMCA in Omagh was the big venue in Tyrone and home to Kenneth Crozier Strong, one of the best defenders of his generation. I had moved ahead of most lads in terms of ability and with regards to my will to win.

"Will we play doubles together Roy?" I asked Roy McLaughlin, one of those strange Protestants that I was now having to deal with and with whom the term 'enemy' was loosely associated with. The following three seasons were great craic as me and Roy tore through various tournaments, winning all the local junior doubles titles. Eventually, this culminated in back to back Tyrone men's doubles titles and an Ulster Boys doubles title against a certain Brian Orr and John Fall. Dirty tactics time was required here. I would call a net or an edge that clearly was not and John Fall would fall for it. He would shout and scream, and Brian would get annoyed at me for annoying John. So on and so on with Roy smiling at me and loving it.

My table tennis career peaked in 1981 with a famous Tyrone Men's title, an Ulster Boys inter-county title, and my third and final international appearance in Bradford. I was the king of the castle and the man solely responsible for it was the one and only Seamus Harkin. At the height of the troubles, he gave up so much of his time to keep us all out of trouble. The only trouble I enjoyed was that of table tennis and the various battles with Ken Strong, Joe Hutton, the Irwin Brothers, Brian Orr, John Fall, and many more. Great times, great memories, but unfortunately, I can no longer share them with Seamus Harkin as he sadly passed from us with cancer in February 2011. Your memory will always burn bright.

"What do you call an Irishman about to fire a gun?" I suddenly shouted at the two lads in the front seat.

"Is this one funny?" Paul asked

"Eamon," I said while laughing.

"Eamon?" asked a very confused Paul Gallagher.

"Aiming," I explained to the lads

"Definitely not funny."

Paul asked where to turn next to which I responded, "turn right Paul, just like normal."

As we were now in Caledon, it was time for me to give the lads another history lesson. They were heading for C's at best. "What is that road on the left famous for?" I asked my two pupils.

"I don't know but have a feeling that we are about to be informed," nodded Sean at Paul.

"That was the venue of the Caledon Protests, organised by Nationalist MP Austin Currie in June 1968. They occupied a house that had been allocated to a 19-year-old unmarried Protestant who happened to be the secretary of a local Unionist politician. A Catholic family with three children had recently been evicted from the house next door. After a few hours, the RUC removed Mr Currie along with two other squatters. Austin Currie was trying to highlight the injustices of the current housing policy. He wanted to draw attention to the system that allowed an individual councillor to give houses to anyone they wished."

"This is similar to the story you told us about how and why Seamus Mallon got into politics," stated Paul. "Indeed lads, we need to start discussing our past, present, and futures," I replied.

"With Boris Johnson and Brexit, I think we are all being sold down the river," shouted Sean.

The rest of the journey to Dublin, apart from our usual pitstop at an Apple Green service station, was taken up with a full discussion on Brexit. I loved this, getting non-confrontational politics out into the open. Not surprisingly, we were almost all in total agreement. The DUP had walked themselves into something dangerous and there was an urgent need for a Nationalist voice at Westminster. The 2017 Westminster election had been a nightmare for Nationalism, with the SDLP losing their last three seats to Sinn Fein, unbelievably including John Hume's Foyle constituency.

5 Leinster Open 19/10/19

After a brief stop at the Apple Green service station to take on board supplies for the rest of the day and to discuss tactics, we finally arrived at the warzone. It was a school in South West Dublin in dire need of an upgrade. The hall itself held the tables but depending on what part of the hall you were in outside light could influence things greatly. You had to play on the same table all day to increase your chances of progress. The tournament itself was actually five tournaments; the men's over 40s (the blue ribbon event), the men's over 50s (my event), the men's over 60s (soon to be my event), the men's over 70s (hopefully I will survive long enough for this to be my event), and the ladies over 40s. The purpose of these tournaments is to select 5 teams for the Home Nations Championships held annually with Dublin being the hosts for September 2020. Being hosts meant that Ireland would supply both A and B teams, so I had to finish at least sixth. The format of today's tournament allows you to enter two events if your age permits it.

The northwest bus, as I always refer to our transport, had entered us three characters into the men's over 40s and men's over 50s. The first of many problems is the fact that the over 40s is played first and the question of how serious you should take it. You want to qualify out of your initial group of three or four people and get knocked out by one of the top seeds. Getting knocked out too early isn't good but a long run in the over 40s would raise fitness issues later on.

The fun started in the over 40s with an interesting group including the Wexford Viking Brian Devereux and Galway's very own Robbie Gavin. First up was my match against the Wexford Viking. Brian is good craic and an all-round nice guy, his nickname comes from his role as an extra on the TV drama 'The Vikings'. He has a long beard and somehow has an attractive wife Sabrina who happens to be Russian. Sabrina also plays table tennis and has become more Irish than the Irish themselves.

For some strange reason, the Viking was using pimples which gave me a fighting chance against him. As I had never beaten him before it took me a while to convince myself that today was the day… Of course, it wasn't and I lost 3-2. If only I disliked the guy.

With two people qualifying from the group there was still hope. But again, I had never beaten Robbie Gavin either. Twenty minutes later I emerged as a 3-2 victor and all I needed was for the Viking to slay Robbie. As I watched their match unfold, I was horrified as I slowly worked out in my head that if Robbie wins then we would have all won one match and lost another. Ten minutes later as Robbie was shaking the hand of the defeated Viking I walked over and congratulated both. Neither of these clowns could count and had no idea who had qualified. Me being super intelligent and reasonably good with numbers (Greatest financial advisor on James Street Omagh) I explained the whole entire process to the two likely lads. Needless to say, I accused both of them of a complete fix, my temporary dislike for Brian only lasted eleven seconds. Countback is the process players use if all have won an equal number of matches. It goes next to sets won and eventually points won.

How had the rest of the North West lads done? Sean 'the Chopper' would chop no more in the 40s, but the Donegal Slapper had somehow reached the last eight. This was where the fun can really start as me and Sean fought over who would become Paul's coach. Paul was up against the number one seed Daryl Strong, son of the man I destroyed in the semi-finals of the Tyrone Men's Championship back in 1981. Paul won the second game, but Daryl eventually won 3-1. My coaching amounted to a bit of pointing and some hand gesturing but all to no avail. Paul sacked me as his coach yet again as we all headed off to get ready for the real competition.

Because of my non-attendance at the Irish Classification, I was now seeded fourth in my group, this could mean disaster. Phil Shaw, Dave Cunningham, and Denis Kelly were my three opponents. Fortunately, I had a 100% record against the three of them. I manipulated things so that I would play Phil first. As he was due to play in the over 60s semi-finals, I knew his mind would be set on that. I also knew that he knew he would beat both Dave and Dennis. Bingo, my plan worked to perfection. I won 3-0 but that little smile on his face told me that he saw what I was up to. I went on to beat Dennis but struggled against Dave Cunningham, finally winning 3-2.

Keeping an eye on the rest of the hall, Paul had continued his good form, and Derry head Sean 'the chopper' also progressed to the quarter-finals. If you win your group, you play someone that came runner up in their group. Needless to say, my nemesis was waiting for me in the last sixteen, one Mark McAlister, namely '10 bats', namely 'the

Octopus'. This man is my shadow, no matter where I go, I will always meet him. Mark loves table tennis so much that he turns up everywhere to play, even my own f...king club. He lives in Cookstown and is the second-best player in Tyrone with Rodney McKirgan being third best. I introduced country membership for all those living approximately twenty miles outside of Omagh. Mark '10 bats' McAlister was the first to pay. Paul and Sean are also country members and play alongside myself and Anthony White in our A team in the Greystone League.

All joking aside, that is the man I most enjoy playing. He has top serves and a vicious Joe Hutton loop. Yes, the Joe Hutton that I beat in the 1981 Tyrone men's championship finals. But best of all he plays with pimples and I always fancy my chances when fit. The usual pattern emerged as we yet again headed into the fifth and deciding set. As I lost this set, I will not discuss it any further than to just say that the better player on the day won.

With the day over it was back to being coach again, a position I again gave myself without asking for Paul's consent. Kieran Burke ripped through Paul who was ignoring my pleading for him to be more offensive. Sean fell to one of the big two meaning our day was nearly done.

We watched on as Pat McCloughan defeated Kevin Mackey to make it one title each out of two tournaments played. My brain went into overdrive to work out the provisional rankings after two events, which isn't an easy task as every event has different ranking points attached. Please do not ask why.

Position	Player	Tournaments Played	Ranking points
1	Pat McCloughan	2	380
1	Kevin Mackey	2	380
3	Kieran Burke	2	240
3	Nejobsa Gabric	2	240
5	Paul Gallagher	2	200
5	Phil Shaw	2	200

Selected others

Position	Player	Tournaments Played	Ranking points
8	Sean McAnaney	2	160
8	Mark McAlister	2	160
20	Des Flanagan	1	70

It Takes Balls…

6 Journey Home From Leinster Open

As we headed for home I was back in my rightful position, upfront with Paul. If you are in the backseat on the way to Dublin, you are automatically in the front on the way home. This is a little system that I introduced for all league matches to avoid issues regarding egos and who should sit where. *"Des Flanagan and ego, who would ever have thought that those words would go in the same sentence?"* I responded to Bad Des with, "you have been absent today."

"No need to annoy you today as you are going nowhere fast. International table tennis will just have to stay buried deep in your memory bank Desmond." He had a point.

"I think I will have to award myself player of the tournament," shouted Paul with a smug grin on his face, two-quarter final appearances, and heading straight for the Irish over 50's A team. Which of you two are buying the coffees and the Magnums?"

"What is the rule if none of us play each other?" asked Sean, backing his buddy up.

"Ok, ok lads, I will buy the coffees and the Magnums this time. But only because Paul is driving and certainly not because he is a better player," I stated.

Normally if one player in the car loses to another player in the car, then the loser buys coffee. If there is a second match played between the occupants, that loser buys the Magnum ice creams. What you really want is the other two clowns to play each other in both competitions so you get both for free. No matter how well your business may be going, there is nothing better than tucking into a lovely expensive Magnum, all washed down with an Apple Green coffee.

"Do you still think you have any chance of joining Paul in the Irish team this year Des?" The tone of the question was immediately interpreted as a wind-up and suitably ignored.

"Jesus Des, even I am in a better position than you," continued the Derry wind up artist in the back.

I went on the counterattack. "Sean, why don't you go back to your 'find a Chinese wife' websites?"

"She is only a friend, as I always tell you, Des."

"Don't bluff a bluffer Sean."

"Have you got the football scores there?" shouted Sean trying to change the subject. At this point, I could detect a slight smile from Paul as he continued at exactly one hundred kilometres per hour, or sixty-two and a half miles an hour to us non-compliant Europeans.

"Celtic 6-0 Ross County, Kilmarnock 2-1 Livingston"

"Nobody is interested in that shite that is played in Scotland," shouted Sean.

"FC Union Berlin 2-0 SC Freiburg
FC Augsburg 2-2 Bayern Munich
Fortuna Dusseldorf 1-0 Mainz
RB Leipzig 1-0 Wolfsburg

Werder Bremen 1-1 Hertha Berlin
Dortmund 1-0 M Gladbach"

"Why do you always drone on about German football?" Sean asked in a non-polite manner. "He just drones on Sean," added Paul with that little grin on his face.

"The Huber," I shouted. "Martin Huber from Lautenbach."

"Are we going to have to listen to another of your endless rantings about nothing in particular?" Sean asked, beginning to focus on his 'find a Chinese bride' websites again.

I met Martin Huber on my first day at Aston University in October 1981 where I had gone to study Business Studies with Computer Science. We were staying on the same floor in one of the city centre tower blocks on campus. The Huber was to be our main player alongside Cormac O'Hare from Milford on our famous 'Oslo 81' 5 a side football team. In recent years we have met up every second year normally due to football.

"Did I ever tell you about me and McCusker and the Huber at the Bayern Munich vs Celtic Champions League game in Munich 18th October 2017?"

Sean butted in, "Paul can you put on the news there please so I can get the English football scores."

Paul returned with "Do you not want to listen to that beautiful story Des has in store for us?" No was the prompt answer to that.

Everton 2-0 West Ham United
Aston Villa 2-1 Brighton and Hove Albion
Bournemouth 0-0 Norwich City
Chelsea 1-0 Newcastle United
Leicester City 2-1 Burnley
Tottenham Hotspur 1-1 Watford

Wolverhampton 1-1 Southampton
Crystal Palace 0-2 Manchester City

Select other scores

Leeds United 1-0 Birmingham City
Stoke City 2-0 Fulham
Clochnacuddin 0-7 Brora

"What was the Liverpool score?" asked Sean.

"Don't know, I wasn't listening to that boring football stuff," countered Paul

"They are playing tomorrow you clown; do you know anything about football Sean?"

"Derry City are and were always better than that Omagh Town F.C lot," responded Sean to my insult.

"Hi, hi, be careful there big boy, do not under any circumstances start slagging my Omagh Town."

"What year did they fold Des?"

"Two thousand and f…king five Sean, and you can now apologize." I was getting quite irritated.

"Coffee time children, did you say you were buying the player of the tournament Coffee and a Magnum?" Paul said, trying to defuse the situation.

Twenty minutes later as we climbed back into the car, me with my finances depleted, and Paul piped up, "No more football lads."

"What will we talk about now?"

"Brexit for fucks sake"

Around about the time of this conversation Boris Johnson was sending his now-famous un-signed letter to Donald Tusk asking for an extension to Article 50. Now I must admit that this particular action fell straight into the 'smart ass' category and it was the first time that I had felt any sort of admiration for our 'new great leader.'

"Lads, do you realise that David Cameron must have been the first British Conservative prime minister that had to resign for actually following through on a manifesto promise, calling that referendum," I exclaimed.

"When exactly was that referendum?" Paul asked. It was 23/6/16 to be precise.

"Just under 52% of the UK population voted for something they did not understand," I stated. "Scotland voted 62% against, London was 60% against, we were 56% against, and in Wales, 52% were for it. I am never going to go to Wales again after that performance, what even is the point of Wales?"

"He is off," said Sean. "What do you think will happen next?"

"Theresa May calling that election in June 2017 was some disaster. Imagine allowing the DUP to hold the balance of power. Do they realise how dangerous it will be if the Good Friday Agreement is undermined?"

"What do you mean Des?" asked the Donegal slapper.

"At the moment I live very comfortably in 'N. Ireland' and I am very happy looking after everybody's money and I'm reasonably happy with current affairs. I can class myself as Irish and always travel with my Irish passport. The UK and Ireland are all part of the EU, so the same rules apply to us all. Once you have one part of our island inside and the other part outside, that changes things. It will undermine my Irishness and I will not be happy. Remember, I am a very soft nationalist. The thing that really annoys me is that the DUP goes on about a large percentage of Northern nationalists will not vote for a United Ireland in a border poll. Balls, balls, and more balls to that. They have antagonised us so much that every single soft nationalist will vote for a United Ireland. However, it is not a united Ireland that I want but instead an agreed Ireland." More on this later.

Over the next half, an hour our deliberation on Brexit continued with our isolation and lack of Nationalist voice in Westminster again taking centre stage.

As we headed by Newry, on through Markethill, I nodded towards Seamus Mallon's house. I had recently visited him for his six-monthly financial update.

"What are Seamus Mallon's views on Brexit?" asked Paul, with Sean asleep in the backseat. I gave Paul a very short answer even though I had recently spent two hours listening to the man himself discussing every aspect of Brexit on a one to one basis.

As we headed through Armagh I glanced across in the direction of Milford and I drifted off into my own world again. This time it was 'Oslo 81' and Aston University.

With tensions rising and our trip to Brussels nearly upon us, I started thinking that anywhere but the North was the answer regarding third-level education. I walked into Rodney Tierney's office (my careers teacher) and asked him for one of those prospectuses for any English university. He stretched out behind himself without looking and grabbed one. It turned out to be that of Aston University, the second university in Birmingham, just off the city centre. With that level of research, I decided upon Aston University. Everything in 1981 was potluck so why not my university choice.

Within a couple of days of arriving at Aston University, we had gathered a motley crew of Irish and non-English people into a loose gang. The Huber was soon to be Head of Overseas Affairs and the subject of entering a five a side football team arose. Although I was a Nationalist rather than a Republican it still meant England and the English were fair game. I went to town and my brilliance would soon come to the fore.

We made an oath. "We, the undersigned, agree to enter a five a side football team with the promise that no English person can ever play for us." The first three signatures were Des Flanagan from Omagh, Cormac O'Hare from Milford Armagh, and Martin Huber from Lautenbach West Germany, soon to be just Germany. All we needed was a suitably inappropriate name.

"Maggie Thatcher, Princess Diana, Winston Churchill, your boys took one hell of a beating," was all I could remember of the greatest bit of commentary I had ever heard after an English defeat. Norway 2-1 England in the World Cup qualifier in Oslo September 1981.

And with that 'Oslo 81' was born. In the coming weeks, everything happened. We managed to get a tape recording of the famous speech and proceeded to play it before every match. This led to the ridiculous situation of us getting a player sent off before a match. A temperamental Scottish student with the name of 'Tam' who was ancient (approximately 40 years old). 'Mature' he was not but he shared a love of beating the English. In another match, we played a French goalkeeper who we quickly nicknamed 'dropsy'. We were frequently short of a fifth player so many a lady played for us. The competition was played and out of every team, we came bottom, though our only victory was against the eventual champions.

After sixteen weeks of 'study', my career was over at Aston and I was heading home. Computer Science had proved to be slightly too mathematical for me and Liverpool University and Law was set to be my next adventure. Amazingly with me off the team, Oslo 81 improved dramatically. So in love with the team was Cormac O'Hare that he settled in Perton, Wolverhampton, and continued playing for them well into his thirties. Unfortunately,

Cormac is one of my mates that no longer talks to me. Our last get together was on 20th April 2002. I know the date because I had travelled over to see Birmingham City's last game of the season against Sheffield United, resulting in a 2-0 home win for the Blues. All I can remember is that words were exchanged in the early hours after a long day of refreshments. Did I slag him off for breaking our covenant and playing English players or was it something else? Anyhow big lad if it was my fault, I am still sorry. To this day I still have a Norwegian flag and hope to bring it along with yourself and the Huber to Oslo.

Football and table tennis were my fond memories of Aston University. Our team was Birmingham City because Aston Villa had just won the old European Cup by beating the Huber's Bayern Munich with a Peter Withe goal. "Shit on the Villa, Shit on the villa tonight" is still occasionally sung.

7 Journey To Ulster Open

Ulster Open 16/11/19 Ballymena

Again with the routine. Three pairs of socks, new table tennis shoes with go-fast stripes down the side, spare pair of shoes, two pairs of shorts, three shirts to make me look fit, a tracksuit, two hand towels, two bats, and a water pistol just in case it all kicks off.

There are now two main reasons why I follow this strict routine. Firstly, many years ago I turned up at a very important tournament without a bat and duly got destroyed as I could not find a bat in the hall with my special and probably illegal anti-loop rubber on it. More embarrassingly, I recently spent half an hour getting ready to meet up with the lads in Omagh to go for a cycle. I had my routine. Cycling shoes, cycling shorts, undervest, top, glasses, helmet, and Garmin watch. Great, headed off to Omagh but just before we set off I realised I had forgotten the most important item for a cycle…yes, no bike with me. This is why I describe myself as 'allegedly intelligent'.

Today the plan would be different. We were virtually playing at home if you call playing at Wellington Presbyterian

Church Hall playing at home. It was the Ulster Open so the southern numbers would be down, and opportunities would present themselves. The other big difference was that I was travelling alone so my need to 'entertain' the boys was gone.

Up the hill, past the local Orange Hall with its Union Jack upside down (Somebody will be in trouble), down Glenpark road, left along St Mary's Road, left through Killyclogher, left and out onto the Cookstown Road, and time to relax. Did I bring that green and white hooped Mexican club shirt that resembles a Celtic shirt just to annoy Norman McBride? Maybe the next time. If I got knocked out early today, I was going to torture Norman, our host regarding Celtic's bid for 9 in a row. To those that do not know him, Norman McBride was the organiser of the day's tournament. A Rangers and Ballymena United fan and a really nice guy, something that I will never say to him.

It was not long before my mind had suddenly jumped back to 1982. I wondered what had happened that year. Firstly, the marathon craze had started and of course, a wee notion entered my head that running a marathon would be a good idea. To put myself under pressure I entered the Foyle Festival Marathon in the city of Derry prior to doing any training whatsoever. The fact that the event was exactly six weeks away did not seem like an obvious problem. That quickly changed when I pulled up and stopped after 3 miles on my first training run. The next day I walked, ran, walked, and ran about 6 miles into the Omagh library to study all the recently published books on how to run a marathon. This process of headless chicken training continued up until the day of the marathon… then disaster struck.

Sunshine… six weeks of training in the rain, snow, sleet, and more rain, then on the morning of the bloody marathon it was blue skies. To this day I be in the city of Derry almost every week because of work, and the sun rarely appears. Obviously, I did not know what lay ahead of me. The whole project was one of buck stupidity. But I had a plan, not a very good one but a plan nonetheless. I would find an attractive female runner and stick to her like glue. Four hours with me or just under as per my plan and, well, she was bound to fall for me. Seriously, I thought this was a sensible and very feasible plan. All started well. The most I had run-up to that point was sixteen miles so I went easy enough until that point and the plan after that was to just hang on.

It was round about the sixteen-mile mark that I found my attractive female or, as it turned out, Mr. Patsy Arkinson, a Catholic priest. It is amazing where you can find a Catholic priest especially when you are not looking for one. How do I even know or even remember his name? I went to school with his little brother Seamus Arkinson, who used to be the second-best financial advisor on James Street before he moved out and started expanding to become my biggest rival in the world of finances. Amazingly, things were still going reasonably well by the time I reached the Caw Roundabout. Someone was shouting that we were on target for a 3:30 marathon time. I was praying for a sub-4-hour marathon and now with a Catholic priest beside me, what could possibly go wrong?

The next time you happen to be at the Caw Roundabout heading back towards the Limavady Road, please look at that gradient and think of poor wee undertrained Des and that mountain. After about 100 meters Patsy started panting and the sun was bouncing up off the melting tarmac. Anybody with water bottles or even hoses were lifesavers. On we struggled, this marathon was going to be run nonstop or so I thought. Two minutes later I was in the gutter and I mean in the gutter. That climb, foot by foot was horrendous. Finally, we peaked Everest and started our slow descent. Not a word was uttered by Mr. Flanagan for the next hour apart from crying for water and help. Somehow, I was in the Bogside and all I could see were pints of harp. Some kind souls were actually offering me free pints. Temptation indeed. I finally hit the wall, a term I would only learn about years later when I increased my training programme from six to nine weeks. We were now nearly there. Without the support of the Bogside locals, I simply would never have finished.

After three hours and fifty-seven minutes myself and my very attractive running partner, AKA Patsy Arkinson stumbled over the line. A sub-four marathon in six weeks of headless chicken planning. Some achievement. I was a marathon runner. Little did I know then but it would take a further twenty-one years of disasters before I would finally beat this time.

It wasn't long before the troubles and our past was to interrupt my journey to Ballymena.

What struck me next on my drive to the Ulster Open was the old Manchester City scarf hanging from the Teebane memorial. Without thinking I was upon the site in the North that I find the most difficult to pass, but it was the Manchester City scarf that had made me actually pull the car over and actually stop.

William Gary Bleaks (25)

Cecil James Caldwell (37)

Robert Dunseith (25)

David Harkness (23)

John Richard McConnel (38)

Nigel McKee (22)

Robert Irons (61)

Oswald Gilchrist (44)

I was now about 17 miles out of Omagh heading to Ballymena via Cookstown and Toome. I had stopped the car for the first time ever at the Teebane bombing memorial. Doubly difficult to fathom is the fact that someone in their wisdom had decided to vandalise the memorial.

The Teebane massacre happened on 17th January 1992. Eight men died and six others were injured when the IRA exploded a roadside bomb. Those caught up in the attack were all construction workers travelling in a van on their way home from Omagh. The IRA claimed that they were targeted because they had been working on repairs at the British Army base in Omagh.

The reason why that date is important to me is because in November 1992 I started my career in the financial services industry. Every week since early 1992 I have passed that sight. Today, however, was the first time that I have pulled my car in to pay my respects. As I have now became a soft nationalist this memorial is horrific to look at. Over the years I have tried to put myself into the position of people with different views than mine, Unionists, Loyalists, and Republicans. I can understand why people have done certain things even though I totally disagree with their actions. But this, this was cold-blooded sectarian murder. This is crazy stuff; this is what causes civil war. I have done things in the past that I totally regret and some of it gnaws away at me. How must these people feel? Some people will be proud of their actions, but many will be suffering in silence.

I have always held a belief that N. Ireland needs a South African style 'Peace and Reconciliation' forum. A forum that would allow people to come forward and simply state what happened to them and their families. Additionally, if people wanted to come forward and tell what they did and why they believe they did it, surely this would help us all going forward. For those that suffered the most during the Troubles and especially those who have received no justice whatsoever (Like the Teebane families) this process would be very tough. People are constantly trying to rewrite our shared history, but surely this history belongs to the people themselves.

I am aware of the Bradley/Eames Consultative group. This had the potential to deliver what I am simply asking for. As usual with this part of the world, it ran into politics and opposing political forces

This group said that such a commission would take over the work currently carried out by the Police Ombudsman and the Historical Enquiries Team, a specialised police unit set up to investigate unsolved killings throughout the troubles. The group sparked controversy when it suggested paying £12,000 to all the families of victims of violence, including paramilitaries.

The group created further controversy in early 2008 by suggesting that the troubles could be officially classified as a war. Relatives of security force victims argue that this would undermine the sacrifice of their relatives during the darkest days of the troubles. Their relatives were often shot when off duty and unable to defend themselves. Their opponents were not obeying the rules of war as commonly understood.

Former Secretary of State Shaun Woodward was against such payment.

The UUP called the proposal a "One-sided truth

commission."

The Alliance party believed that the legacy commission should be at the centre of future structures.

The DUP said that justice is "Integral to our Constitution" but believed the commission could "become a vehicle which will prevent innocent families having their day in court."

Sinn Fein called for the creation of an "independent international truth commission" which could be funded by a group such as the UN.

The SDLP wanted a "Re-working of current arrangements" to merge the Historical Enquiries Team and the Police Ombudsman in an independent body.

As I got ready to get back into my car, I was still thinking that a peace and reconciliation forum is something seriously worth considering, organised by the people for the people. Start it slowly and let it grow its own legs. The Manchester City scarf was also on my mind. It obviously belonged to one of the victims. Which one? It was the old-style 'Maine Road' City scarf and by the look of it, is a scarf that has actually been at matches.

My mind was now racing at a hundred miles an hour. Why do we never hear the voices of normal people on the radio stations? There are plenty of people like me that hold moderate views within both the Nationalist and Unionist communities. I deal with them every day of the week. For God's sake, I talk politics with them every day of the week, and the worst thing that happens is that we slightly disagree. But that is the nature of politics.

Part of my mind was trying to race off to 1982 and the next big event to affect me. Namely the Falklands War. It became almost the first-ever televised war and me and my Da watched it together. However, this period between Universities also allowed my first bit of entrepreneurship to appear, although I can guarantee not everybody will be happy regarding its nature.

The Falklands War (Guerra de las Malvinas) was a 10-week undeclared war between Argentina and the United Kingdom in 1982 over two British dependant territories in the South Atlantic: The Falklands and its territorial dependencies of South Georgia and the South Sandwich Islands.

The conflict began on the 2nd of April when Argentina invaded and occupied the Falkland Islands, followed by an invasion of South Georgia the next day. On the 5th of April, the British government dispatched a naval task force to engage the Argentine Navy and Air Force before making an amphibious assault on the islands. The conflict lasted 74 days and ended in an Argentine surrender on the 14th of June, returning the islands to British control. In total 649 Argentine military personnel, 255 British military personnel, and three Falkland islanders died in the hostilities.

Back in the land of many names we had split down party lines. The Unionists were 100% behind the empire while the Republicans favoured the Argentine army, and the Nationalists were confused.com. I reacted immediately to the fighting, using my father's contacts to order as many Argentinian football shirts as I could. As a huge football fan, I was already working on my football shirt collection.

Only about twenty of these shirts ever arrived and I quickly sold them, doubling my money. Instantly a second and more substantial order was placed. Unfortunately, this never arrived as everybody else twigged on to this scheme, or else the British supplier twigged our game. Overnight every Nationalist and Republican town in the North seemed to have set up independent supporters clubs for the Argentinian national football team. Needless to say, I never wore the shirt but was happy with the profit made. To this day I still refer to the Falklands as 'Las Malvinas' and Malbec is my favourite red wine. Maradona and the 'hand of god' was Argentina's revenge for defeat in Las Malvinas. Sport is always the answer.

As my car stopped at Wellington Presbyterian Church, I was ready for battle. However, I was already completely knackered. Not a good start.

It Takes Balls…

8 Ulster Open 16/11/19

"Good morning Norman, Rangers going well this season?"

"Didn't take you long to start Mr. Flanagan," retorted Norman.

"This year we will do a 9 in a row and next year Celtic will be the first team in the history of Scottish football to win 10 titles in a row."

"Never."

I changed the subject. "I hope I get a good draw today."

Normal bluntly stated, "No chance."

"Where is Sean today Paul?" I asked the Donegal head.

"China, do you ever listen to a single thing he says to you?" was rudely thrown my way by Paul. "He is on tour in china with his company TitanicDance."

"Is he meeting his Chinese girlfriend when he is over there?"

"I presume so."

This tournament had the same format as the last one, starting with the over 40's groups. Myself and Paul both qualified out of our groups and immediately got knocked out in the last 16. This gave us the opportunity to talk some nonsense and watch the later stages of the over 40s. Paul had also pointed out the fact that we were in the same group as each other for the over 50s. This was not necessarily good news as I hate playing him, only because I think very highly of him and find it hard to motivate myself (my excuse anyway).

Daryl Strong beat Mr. Molzenberger from County Cork via Germany in one semi and Rory Scott, based in England, beat 'fast' Phil Wallace from Belfast in the other. During the day Paul was constantly talking with Roy Scott regarding tactics and also to avoid me. In the final Rory upset the odds defeating Daryl. I believe that this was the first time in four years that Daryl had lost a vets table tennis match in Ireland. Needless to say, the Donegal Slapper claimed all the credit and awarded himself the title 'Coach of the Year'.

With us both having won our opening match in our three-man over 50s groups we had both qualified. Although we were not travelling together that day the match to follow would be classed as a Coffee match and would determine who would get the initial abuse on our next journey to Dublin.

I would love to describe how I won the match but I can't because I got stuffed 3-0 and it wasn't even that close. Now it all depended on the luck of the draw. I was set to play the winner of a group while Paul was set to play a runner up.

"You will have Phil Shaw and I'll have Jeremy Lappin," grinned Paul about twenty minutes later. We locked heads together to discuss tactics. Although I had never lost to Phil Shaw it would be a classic 50/50 game. Paul should easily beat Jeremy eight or nine times out of ten.

"Remember you stuffed him 11-8, 11-4, and 11-8 when we played our B team last week." Jeremy is based in

Letterbreen which is about 35 miles from Omagh but has availed of our country membership scheme.

I watched as the Donegal Slapper sat there and did nothing. Clearly, Jeremy was highly motivated, getting stuffed in a league match must have clearly annoyed him. Before long Paul was beaten 3-1. This put me in a difficult position as Paul is a very good mate of mine and I have a great time for Mr. Lappin, it didn't seem appropriate to step in and coach Paul to victory so I didn't bother. The other issue is my need to get on the Irish team and Paul is a major obstacle on my road to glory. My hopes didn't seem great as I hadn't recovered from stopping at Teebane and I had barely hit a ball all day.

Chop the arse off his serves into my backhand and high loop him off the table, let on that you do not like him, and get the big dog firing on all cylinders. Surprisingly, the master plan was working and before long I was 2-0 and 9-6 points up in the third set. Phil Shaw however loves a good fight and today he was not ready to go home. Suddenly it was 2-1 sets and 9-9 points with Phil serving. If I lost this game Phil would rip my head off in the fifth and deciding game. Balls, balls, and more balls. He placed a long serve down my backhand, but I had moved early and fast (I know, not too fast) and just hit it. Match point, harder serve down my backhand which I chopped to death. Phil pushed the ball back and I just hit hard and hoped… Victory, I was holding my hands in the air. Phil Shaw is a pure gentleman in defeat, but I recognised that look that said "Next time Flanagan."

Quarter final vs Branislav Jakovetic.

He is a very intelligent player. He is also a very interesting character and many many a conversation we have had. History is normally what we talk about. Having recently read Ante Nazar's book 'The Croatian War of Independence', I had a hundred more questions. If people think the North is complicated, they should read all about the breakup of Yugoslavia. Whilst reading this book I was also watching BBC documentaries on the same subject. Reading books, watching a documentary, and no exams. That is what I call real history.

The match itself was an epic. I led 2-1 with Paul 'Coach of the Year' actually helping to keep me focused. At 2-2 Paul kept me calm and instructed me to go on the all-out attack especially now with the big dog coming into form. Ran away with the fifth and deciding set before Branko nearly killed me with a Russian bear hug.

Semi-Final vs David Pemberton.

My mind was racing but Paul was beginning to earn his title. My mind was also heading back to my international days and there was little I could do to stop it.

1979	1980	1981
Intermediate Boys	Senior Boys	Senior Boys
Michael Greene	Alan McCormick	Richard McWilliams
Richard McWilliams	Richard McWilliams	Alan McCormick
Peter Barry	David Pemberton	Desmond Flanagan
John O'Connell	Peter McCabe	Mark Irwin
Desmond Flanagan	Desmond Flanagan	S Flavin
		E Byrne

'Told you he was an international, told you he was a better player

than you. Forget it, Des, you have no chance," taunted Bad Des who had reappeared into my life. "Piss off" I shouted back.

"Who are you talking to now?" exclaimed Paul.

"Nobody, nobody Paul."

"Des, you must go at him from the very start. Remember that he is left-handed, and you haven't played a leftie all day. Chop his first serve and attack down his forehand… and whatever you do, do not upset Mr. Dave Pemberton."

"Okay Des, scream at him if you win the first point," suggested Bad Des.

Right, let's go. Coach of the Year was bang on and soon I was leading 2-1 and 8-7. Get this done. Bang, I lost the set 11-8. I hadn't beaten Dave Pemberton since my comeback. Bad Des was having a field day. Remarkably in the next 5-10 minutes, I played the best table tennis since returning to the game, reaching levels not attained since 1981. Dave was also gracious in defeat, maybe because I only let one roar out of me and that was when I fired a non-returnable big dog down the line to win the point, set, and match. Paul Gallagher was really in line for a raise.

Final vs Kevin Mackey

Although I also hadn't beaten Kevin Mackey since my return, I strangely believed that I had the game to beat him. I was down 2-0 very easily and not long after that Pemberton was in Kevin's corner. The third game was much closer but to no avail with a final score of 12-10. If only I had pinched that third set, who knows. I shook hands with Kevin and his coach. I duly walked over and shook Paul's hand and sacked him on the spot. You waster, no bonus for you. Paul was standing there with the biggest grin on his stupid face.

Coach of the Year indeed. "I can only work with what I have got," he announced to the onlooking crowd (12 people). Paul got the biggest clap of the night.

Although slightly annoyed that I had not gone all the

way, I was buzzing. I even went over to Norman to let him rattle on about his beloved Rangers and how this was the year.

My brain was quickly working out what this all meant.

Over 50s Provisional Irish Vets Ranking after 3 events

Position	Player	Tournaments played	Ranking Points
1	Kevin Mackey	3	580
2	Pat McCloughan	3	380
3	Nebojsa Gabric	3	330
4	Paul Gallagher	3	290
5	Mark McAlister	3	270
5	Philip Shaw	3	270

Selected Others

7	Dave Pemberton	3	250
9	Des Flanagan	2	230
13	Sean McAnaney	2	160

9 Journey Home From Ulster Open

Pulling out of Ballymena I was in good form as I had now proved that I could compete at the top level of over 50's table tennis in Ireland. With no one in the car, the usual post-mortem did not take place. No winding up Sean or Paul but at least I would not have to buy the coffee on the way home. It was almost 8 o clock which meant it was time to get the football scores, with extra attention being given to the Man City result after that morning.

European Championship qualifying games were being played today rather than English and Scottish premiership football. Scotland beat Cyprus 2-1 in Cyprus and N. Ireland continued their excellent form under Michael O'Neil with a nil-nil draw at home to the Netherlands. The following days would produce some brilliant videos of the Dutch fans walking out to Windsor Park in one large group. Finally, an Orange parade in Belfast that nobody could object to. If we ever reach normality in the North, the twelfth of July could become a centrepiece in attracting tourists from all over the world. I like to look at the positives in most situations and this is a great opportunity for all of us to move forward.

"' *Orangefest' indeed, we could put a Sinn Fein minister in charge of this one,*" suggested Bad Des.

Now sitting with a coffee on my lap I was glancing at the Irish League scores. This is something that I have rarely done since Omagh Town F.C folded in 2005. Before moving to Dunmullan I had lived beside the ground at St Julian's Road or 'Stadia Julianno' as I had labelled it due to Channel 4's coverage of the Italian football. I loved going there on a Saturday and meeting up with the lads. McCreadie would never bore you and the football club was giving local lads a chance. It was also a feeder club for Derry City FC which we were reasonably happy about. It was a good way for young talent to work its way through.

To this day I still partly blame Sinn Fein for the collapse of 'The Town' which is probably not really fair. However, it is my head and my little brain works independently of reason when it needs to. Sinn Fein had no interest in a 'foreign sport' being played locally. No grants were made available to upgrade etc. However, there were other real reasons. A large percentage of people living in Omagh are from the surrounding towns and villages where Gaelic Football is the dominant sport. They would prefer to support their own parish teams. What a job they have done. Whilst driving around the north for my work I've seen that the standard of the pitches and facilities of most GAA clubs is excellent. They obviously have people in the right places especially regarding fundraising and understanding the various grant systems. Omagh Town was always chasing its tail and without Pat McGlinchey would have fallen years earlier. I still have the Manchester United and Chelsea programmes from those three charity matches. Fond, fond memories indeed. What role would Flanagan and McCusker be performing today if 'The Town' were still playing? A question that always arises if we ever get to the fifth pint.

With football on my mind I was straight back to my University days in both Aston University in Birmingham and Liverpool University. Table tennis, football, table tennis, football, and last minute.com study to scrape a third-class honours degree in law. Aston Villa won the league in 80-81, followed by Liverpool in 81-82, 82-83 and 83-84. Everton won it in 84-85. After I returned to civilization Liverpool again won in 85-86, followed by Everton in 86-87. Regarding football, I for one was in the right place at the right time. Also during this period, Liverpool would beat AS Roma on penalties to win the European Cup in May 1984 and Everton would win the old Cup Winners Cup in 1985 against Rapid Vienna 3-1 in Rotterdam. This period is also known for what happened at our old stomping ground of The Heysel Stadium in Brussels on the 29th May 1985. The next morning would be my last ever law exam. Fate plays a role in all our lives and I am a great believer in this, when it rolls your way you must grab it.

I have countless memories of football matches that I attended during this period and a few now started popping back into my head. In no particular order; Celtic vs Rapid Vienna on Wednesday 12th of December, greatest atmosphere ever at an Old Trafford match ending in defeat. Milk Cup final and replay, Liverpool vs Everton on 28/3/84 at Maine Rd (PS. I always support Everton in the Merseyside derby). The night before the cup final at Wembley we had stayed above a pub near Wembley Stadium. My mate's father was the landlord. The next day three hours before kick-off all the buses from Liverpool arrived. Most of the buses were mixed, no not Catholics and Protestants but Liverpool and Everton supporters. I was asked to help behind the bar. With

my Everton shirt and Celtic hat, I proceeded to only serve Everton Supporters. The amount of abuse I took that day!
Nottingham Forest vs Glasgow Celtic 23/11/83 UEFA Cup 3rd round 1st leg (0-0 to us but lost the return game 1-0) I ended up in the home end with my Celtic shirt well covered. McCusker and myself met Sir Alex Ferguson that night in a Chinese restaurant. We pulled our seats over and bored the poor man to death for about an hour.
England vs Republic of Ireland 26/3/85 Wembley friendly, lost 2-1 and there was nothing friendly about what was going on outside the ground.

Everton 5-0 Manchester Utd 27/10/84. One two, one two three, one two three four five Nil. We would be singing that night. Peter Reid destroyed Bryan Robson that day.
Everton 3-1 Bayern Munch 24/4/85 in the Cup Winners Cup semi-final second leg. This was the greatest match I was ever at, apart from Celtic 5-1 Rangers. At half time, the Huber's Bayern Munich were one-nil up thus Everton had to score two without reply. Obviously, Everton won. Sharp 48, Andy Gray 75 and Steven 86. The noise from that night still lingers.

My other great love was booming. Finally, I was somewhere where my playing partner was clearly better than I at table tennis. Also, he had the worst temperament I had ever come across, he would fall out with his shadow. Three years in a row we lost in the semi-finals of the British Universities Championships. You had to win your region, then the quarter-finals, and so on. Can somebody please explain how after spending 15 hours a week with this lad for nearly three years, I cannot think of his name? Must have been some fight that last night. Memories of winding up John Fall from Ballymoney come flooding back because I always used those tactics in the deciding doubles. I would start a row and my mate would get furious. Then he became the hulk and upped his game. Fantastic, my levels of gamesmanship were peaking. He was exactly the same size as a certain Jimmy Robinson but prettier. If that gentleman from Liverpool is still alive, I would love to meet you again. Unfortunately, it is neither football nor table tennis that are the abiding memories from my years at Liverpool University but two others. Both of the following stories lead to two of my biggest regrets in life.

Cheerfully we will start with my landlord Fred from Gateacre, Liverpool. Yet again I cannot pull his surname from my memory bank. For two years I lived with Fred about five miles out of Liverpool city centre. Kieran Gibson stayed with us in year two and Kevin Dolan was with us for my final year in university. I loved Fred from the first day I met him. He was retired from the phone exchanges but worked part-time. If I needed to phone home Fred would phone the house and put us through without charge. Towards the end of the second year, my Friday nights would be spent with him down the labour club. The drink was cheap and his old buddies were great craic. Fred was also now in charge of my love life as I had made a complete mess of this. Actually, my love life had never started. 'Failed Womanizer' would sum it up quite well. At this stage, I was more of a nationalist than I am today. I was always ranting on about the North and the British Army and using my little knowledge of the law to 'prove' a point. I still continued to read away at war novels, but this is where fate stepped in. Why was I staying with Fred? It was Fred that the police called that night I was arrested in Liverpool city centre (Innocent or almost innocent – Flanagan's apple bar)

The only thing that Fred did not like was my rantings about the army. After taking about two months to read the book 'A Bridge Too Far' I finally put the book down, but I had a feeling whilst reading it that Fred was constantly watching me.

"What do you think about that Des?" he asked me.

I paused and said something to the effect of "Even though I am no fan of the parachute regiment because of Bloody Sunday, it is dreadful to think that only ten percent of them survived Arnhem."

I watched as tears flowed slowly at first down his ruddy cheeks. Finally, he spoke, "I was one of the ten percent."

I was stunned. This gentle, gentle man had fought in some of the greatest battles of the second world war, in battles that I had constantly read about since being a nipper. No wonder he did not like me giving out about the British Army. Almost at the same time, I understood the cloud that Fred carried around with him all the time. I also had a fair idea what was troubling him. This is not the time nor place but I know one thing, it was no accident that I had ended up living with Fred. Was I there to help Fred or was Fred there to help me, or were we there to help each other? The next couple of months included many great days but also my darkest days.

Regret number one. I did not keep in touch with Fred after I came home. Remember mobile phones and the internet were still many years away. But Fred had actually become my Dad. The man that I could go for a couple of pints with and tell him everything. He never did sort out my love life, but he helped to sort me out or partly so. I am so sorry Fred. I will love you always.

I was sitting at the bottom of the stairs at 5 in the morning when the phone went. It was Uncle John McDermott from Portaferry, my mother's younger brother. "I know John, I know". It had become John's job to phone me with the news that my rock, my mum, was dead. I was days short of my 21st birthday. John had organised and paid for the plane tickets and would pick me up from the airport for that horrendous journey home. Fred of course stepped in and got me to the airport.

1983 was the year the Flanagans and by that, I mean mum and dad, had taken over the An Oige youth hostel just outside Newport Co. Mayo. This was to be the place wherein my mind my mum had been the happiest. Tourists or youth hostel members would arrive and book themselves in for a night or two. The youth hostel overlooks Lough Feeagh which feeds into Furnish and the Atlantic Ocean via Clew Bay. It is the most beautiful place in my world. The locals are of a similar calibre.

It helped that the summer of 1983 was one of those things we rarely got, hot, just like the weather you would expect on the day of a marathon. Mum ran the place like a military operation but without the rules. People were turning up from all over the place and it wasn't long before Mr. McCusker was down to help with my plans. I had just finished one of my years at Liverpool University and was in the mood for messing. It helped that the girls turning up were of a standard we were not used to tackling. Our results with the opposite sex were the only downside of this adventure. Our days would consist of getting or trying to get into Frank Chambers' bar at the lower end of Newport. Frank would sing a few tunes every night and tell a few stories with the same level of truth attached to my father's. Then it was announced that me and McCusker were being put in charge of the hostel for a full week. This must be one of the craziest decisions any set of parents ever came up with. Finally, the day came and my mum and dad headed off. Me and Phil simply could not decide which of us would do what, so we decided we would do nothing remotely called work. The youth hostel system was pretty fool-proof and we were going to test it. The punters would turn up, sign themselves in for a small fee, and set themselves up in one of the bunk beds in one of the dormitories. They had to bring their own sheets or sleeping bags and it was a self-catering operation. The greatest bit was them doing something for the youth hostel in the morning for the reward of a lower overnight charge. Bingo. Every morning Flanagan and McCusker Delegating PLC went to town. Floors need swept, windows cleansed, fire cleaned out, wood brought in, etc. The big problem by day two was obvious. One of us clowns had to get up to deliver the orders/instructions. First committee meeting of Flanagan and McCusker Delegating PLC was not the best. When I pointed out that obvious flaw Mr. McCusker just shrugged his shoulders and gave me that stupid look which he can still do to this day. You can see why he has become a civil servant. Before long I had taken overall military command (again). Transport into Chambers Bar for the cure, transport home (5 miles), cooking (delegated to any guest in lieu of a morning task), and finally transport back to Frank Chambers for nightly music session accompanied by some females. Each morning after delegation and supervisory duties, I would collapse back into bed and Phil would start (eventually) on his pet project, stacking the turf. Phil was actually quite good at this. We did finally get our act together just before mum and dad returned. The best and funniest week in my life.

Thirty years later myself and Phil decided to spend one night in Newport and one night in Westport. As we were booking into the Newport Hotel, which was formerly the Angler's Rest, a middle-aged gentleman coming out of the bar staggered and exclaimed "Jesus no, not Des Flanagan." I immediately recognised him as Neil Masterson who had been in Frank Chamber's bar most nights, "Whatever happened to Phil McCusker?" he asked next, just as Phil emerged from the toilet at reception.

"Hello Neil, I believe it has been thirty years since you last bought us a drink."

"Balls, balls and more balls" could be heard from Neil as he began to realise his quiet night had just been hijacked.

The night after my parents returned to the youth hostel me, Phil and my dad all headed to town in his car to celebrate. The next bit of this book has been censored by Mr. McCusker. If anybody wants to know about Phil's entire driving career and the Angler's Rest, please speak to McCusker himself. I would recommend waiting until he has finished his third pint of Guinness. Losing something you never had comes to mind.

By September it was time to head off back to Liverpool and to my first meeting with Fred. My mum was to take ill towards the end of 1983 and pass away.

To this day those couple of miles between Newport and the youth hostel beside Lough Feeagh are my spiritual home. If I am bothered or simply want a laugh or to reconnect with my mum, I will not be far from there.

All these memories had relieved the tension from the table tennis tournament earlier in the day, but about three miles past Teebane heading towards Omagh the car decided to turn right towards Greencastle and I automatically pulled the car into the right, just beside the graveyard at Rousky.

In Loving Memory

Joey Clarke
Died 12th March 1975
Aged 18 years

Joseph Clarke
Died 16th August 2005

Aged 80 years
Kathleen Clarke
(Nee McDermott)
Died 22nd June 2009
Aged 80 years
Rest in Peace

This time I was in tears. Kathleen was my mum's wonderful sister and Joseph her husband. I had gotten to know them well in Meadowbank, Tullygally, Craigavon when I went up to play table tennis with the local club. Jimmy Robinson, you are a star. This lad and his fellow helpers were doing a Seamus Harkin on the locals and getting as many people off the streets and into sport as possible. I will say nothing about Jimmy getting me into bother in Lurgan and alcohol.

However, it was not that name that had brought the tears but Joey Clarke who had been shot and murdered by the UVF, dying a couple days later on my dad's 45th birthday. The words why, why, and why again keep coming. Him being aged 18 was not helping either. At this stage, my children are 20, 18, and 16. My big lump of a son Keelan is the same age now as Joey was when he was shot dead. 'Is there anything I can do to make sure this never happens again?' are words that bounce round my now wrecked head as I travelled down into Gortin and up home to Dunmullan and my beautiful innocent family.

"You look wrecked," said Edel, handing me my favourite craft beer. "Good day?"

I simply didn't know how to respond.

With Edel gone to bed and me enjoying my second and final beer, I was back to thinking about Mum, Fred, and Liverpool University. After my mum's death, I went on the beer for about a week and I must have been a nightmare to be around. With my finals looming and no work done Fred finally had that word with me.

"You must pass your exams Des."

"Why?"

"To honour your mum."

It was like lightning going through my body. I was so far behind it was not funny. But I slept well that night and after breakfast cooked by Fred, I sat down at the desk in the corner of my bedroom. After about 10 minutes I banged the desk in total frustration, knocking a purple parker pen from somewhere. It had been the last thing my mum had ever given me. I lifted the pen, clicked it, and started my 3-year law degree. The problem was I had four months to do it.

On the wall of my office on James Street sits my law degree. "Gerard Desmond Francis Flanagan. By resolution of the senate to the Degree of Bachelor of Laws with third class Honours on the nineteenth day of July 1985"

To anybody looking at that, a third-class honours is not impressive, but to me, it is probably my greatest achievement and it honours the two people responsible, namely Fred and my Mum.

My second big regret may not even be a regret. I wonder what would have happened if I had approached my entire law degree with the commitment of the last four months. At the end of those months, I had hundreds of questions, but I had not been present when I should have been. Going forward I was going to have to rely on other talents that I didn't realise I had.

Footnote – I also lost contact with Mr. Martin Huber. Two months before my wedding to Edel in May 1996 I wrote to Martin inviting him to our wedding. It had been years since Martin's last letters. Today he is my international right-hand man which doubles my shame of not having contacted Fred, but maybe he had done his job and I had done mine.

It Takes Balls…

10 Journey To Munster Open

On the morning of the fourth of January 2020, I was heading in to pick up Anthony White, an additional person for the journey. Unfortunately, my mind was still awash with our recent shared history and how table tennis was yet again making me think about my past and what we could do to improve the middle ground in Northern Irish politics. The Westminster election had taken place in December and returned Boris Johnson's Conservative Party with a majority of eighty. In the short term, this weakened the DUP's position as they no longer held the balance of power but I was concerned that there was now little to stop Brexit actually going ahead. For years I have been arguing the point that England do not really want anything to do with us. Do the English know how much we cost the exchequer? A conservative figure is £6 billion per annum. With an approximate population of 1.6 million that works out at £3,750 per person, Crazy stuff.

N. Ireland is a first world country but also acts like a third world country. When you ask the local parties how much we cost England annually, you never get an answer.

Although we have some excellent political radio and television programmes, this figure is never discussed. My discussion with my next door neighbours at the Sinn Fein office quickly turns to this £6 billion figure and how a 'united Ireland' will solve it. If I was the public relations person for Sinn Fein I would base myself in England, hire or steal a big green double-decker bus and drive around Westminster with '£115 million more for the NHS' painted on the side. This might change opinions, but what do I know?

So, are we British or Irish? I actually think that we might be neither. England do not want us and the south are ambivalent to say the least. The land of many names that nobody wants! Thus, it might be time for the middle ground to rise up and urgently start discussions on what is actually best for us all. The unionist community needs to start clearly explaining the benefits of staying within the union. Their arguments need to be supported by independent academic research. I urgently need to hear this. Somebody sell it to me please as I am not convinced. I do not want a united Ireland either but rather an agreed Ireland, one that we can all share. These are the thoughts that were wandering around my head as I picked up Anthony and met up with the lads for the next episode of 'Will Des become an international table tennis after 40 years?'

"Anthony, thank God somebody intelligent from Omagh to share our journey with," shouted either the Derry head or the Donegal Slapper. This continued for the next fifteen minutes until I got bored and decided to change the direction of the conversation.

"Sad news about Ronnie Cowan," I stated. Ronnie had died over the Christmas period and I had gone to his wake and his funeral in the Church of Ireland in Dungannon. A large representation from our table tennis community was dwarfed by the even bigger number of Liverpool supporters.

Ronnie was chairman of the local Liverpool Supporters Club and was very much Mr Fixit re tickets. Because I had lived in Liverpool and loved football, me and Ronnie got on like a house on fire. Liverpool's recent 6th European cup win and their march to the league title meant Ronnie was going out on a high. Ronnie was also the man that supported me when I finally started winning Mid Ulster titles again. I had also started sharing my thoughts with Ronnie about our way forward. Without agreeing with me he enjoyed or simply allowed me to rant on. See you sometime Ronnie.

"Will you sort out '10 bats' today?" asked Sean. I had beaten him in the final of our first Greystone grand prix held back in November and felt the tide had turned in my favour. "Yes" was my short answer.

As we approached Markethill, home to Seamus Mallon, Sean brought up the recent Westminster election. "Seamus Mallon must have been overjoyed with the SDLP comeback Des, three seats is much better than none."

"I haven't spoken to him for a couple of months. I know he would have been overjoyed, but the family say that he is not that well."

"Sorry to hear that Des," was the common view in the car. Everybody knew what an important role Seamus Mallon had played in bringing peace back to our land, something I had personally thanked him for on our second meeting.

With political thoughts and my ideas on the way forward, I was keen to see if fate had played any role with any of the lads during the troubles.

"Anthony, where were you on the day of the Omagh Bomb?"

After gathering his thoughts he replied as follows, "Des it was the opening day of the football season and as a Man United supporter I was looking forward with optimism to our continuing renaissance after a lean trophy-less season in 1997-8. This was the season that would end in the treble, the pinnacle of United's achievement under Ferguson. It was my intention to spend the day reclining on the sofa listening to the commentary of our opening fixture home to Leicester City. A routine victory seemed assured.

"I hastened a change to our normal Saturday routine. Paula and I went into town that sunny morning, pushing 9-month-old James in his buggy up and down both sides of High Street and Market Street, doing a bit of shopping and chatting, that was the height of our socialising with a first child.

"We returned home in the early afternoon. As kick-off approached, I rather selfishly tried to encourage Paula to take James out for a walk. She could take him to the library, I suggested, perhaps another walk up the town? She didn't bite.

"The game didn't go exactly to script. Leicester took the lead in the seventh minute through Emile Heskey. As I shuffled uncomfortably on my sofa, a strange thing happened. A gust of wind blew the back door of our house in Killyclogher open. As I got up to close it a dull thud could be clearly heard in the distance. I didn't think that much about it at the time. I closed the door and returned to the sofa. Leicester went two-nil up in the second half, a goal from Tony Cottee. At that moment our neighbour, returning from the town, called over to the house and described the chaotic scenes taking place little more than a mile from our home. Buses and lorries improvised as ambulances were carrying injured and dying shoppers to the hospital. I turned on the radio and heard local councillor Paddy McGowan emotionally relay the carnage he was witnessing in Market Street.

"Man Utd scored two late goals, Sheringham 79 and Beckham 90, to snatch a dramatic draw that day from the jaws of defeat. It was to be a signature trait of the season, late Fergie-time goals. But I couldn't join the exhilaration felt by Man Utd. It didn't seem to matter after all."

I explained to Paul and Sean the significance of what Anthony had just said. Himself, Paula, and baby James had passed by the very site of the Omagh bomb twice that morning. If Paula and James had gone back into town anything could have happened.

"What were you doing that day?" asked Paul.

I recounted my story about bringing Edel back from the wedding in Enniskillen to the hospital, her being met by a river of blood, and how it took years for her to tell her side of the story. Every step she took she feared meeting someone she knew. We had only been married two years and living in our home in Dunmullan one week. As Edel is from Westmeath in the Republic of Ireland she didn't understand any of this, were we any wiser?

I hesitated before telling the next bit of this story as it is not my story. My sister Fiona and her twin daughters Michelle and Louise were in a boutique right beside the bomb. They all walked out uninjured physically, but to this day I wonder what damage was really done. Fiona is a very private person, so I have never asked. Maybe I should revisit this topic.

This was supposed to be a fun day out trying to beat the heads off each other playing stupid table tennis but my head would not let go.

"Sean, what was the story with you and your family on Bloody Sunday?"

Again Sean took a while before answering. "First of all, there are seven of us in the family. Four brothers, two sisters, and myself. I'm the third youngest with a younger brother and a younger sister. The two oldest are my two brothers Sammy and the eldest Bernard. On the day of

Bloody Sunday, my dad was working, and he left strict instructions that no one was to leave home to go to the march. We lived on the Lone Moor Road overlooking the famous Brandywell stadium, the march passed right outside our front door so the temptation was too much for the two eldest guys, so they went off mingling into the crowd. Everyone was so happy and excited. It was only later that mum had noticed that they were gone, but there was no need to worry as everyone seemed so happy. It was only later when the breaking news started coming through on the black and white TV that trouble had broken out in the Bogside and that gunshots had been heard. Then the news was breaking that someone was shot, then another. This news was very worrying as the two eldest were yet to return. Then the younger of the two, Sammy, returned on his own. No great surprise there as Bernard was always the more adventurous of the two. It was long after that before Bernard finally returned. He was in a terrible state as he had been attending to one of the victims, Barney McGuigan, aged 41 and a father of Bernard's close school mate. Barney was shot in the head and sadly died at the scene. I recall Bernard had a scarf on that day and when he returned home it was covered in blood.

"On the days after Bloody Sunday, Derry was like a ghost town. Young guys were easy picking for IRA recruitment, so my dad had a hard job watching over his sons making sure none of us were roped in. Also given the fact that we were living in the heart of Free Derry at the time, it was no easy task for him however we'll always be grateful to him for keeping us sheltered from the hard times that surrounded us. Riots were an everyday activity at the Free Derry barricades, especially at the weekend. We had a caravan just over the border in Donegal, so once school finished on a Friday we were all packed off to Donegal."

Stunned silence, another person's story of near misses. It was bleeding obvious to everyone in the car that we all had been lucky at some point during the troubles. It was also bleeding obvious to us all that if we had been born over the fence our political views would have been different. Understanding this simple fact would be of great help moving forward.

Our tactical meeting at the Applegreen took on more of an R and R role. Rest and recuperation. God knows what the tournament had in store for us, but we all needed a break from the troubles.

11 Munster Open 04/01/20

Brian F…ing Finn, Mark McAlister, and Dave Butler. These are the three names I was staring at on the door's noticeboard for the day's over 50s competition. Needless to say, it was Mr. Finn's name that was getting my full attention. I was seeded two in the group with Brian seeded third, this meant that I would be playing him in the first match in the early afternoon. All three of the other players in the four-man group play with versions of pimples on their bats, but all three have completely different styles. (To all non-table tennis players, the term pimples refers to rubbers with pimples on the outside of the surface. These rubbers grip the ball differently and are used to manipulate your opponent's spin, mainly used by defensive players) What have I done in life to upset God so much that he has put me into the group of death? I wonder do all pimple playing table tennis players all end up in the same part of the hell, hopefully, the really hot bit. I was so distracted by Brian F…ing Finn that the over 40s went by in a daze. I ended up playing Paul Gallagher in the last 16 for the coffee match. With three coffees having to be bought this could be an expensive game. Last time I played Paul I lost but went on a run.

Before long I was walking off the table after a close fought 3-1 defeat to be met by two laughing car 'mates'.

"Americano for me!" shouted Anthony.

"Latte for me!" shouted Sean.

"Fuck!" shouted me.

Next, I had to pretend to be interested when Sean gave me a point by point blow of his great victory against one of the big two, Kevin Mackey. "Pity you didn't beat him in the over 50s" was my feeble response.

"Well done Sean," I eventually muttered.

Anthony, on his first appearance of the year, came in second in his group but lost to 'fast' Phil Wallace in the knockout stages. Paul threw the toys out of the pram when losing to his old county mate Pat McCloughan. Pat is originally from Donegal but now resides in Louth I believe. He is a very good low-risk type of player who uses table tennis loops down both sides. I was gunning for him but have never even taken a single set off him, never mind actually beaten him. Sean lost to the eventual winner of the day's over 40s tournament, Daryl Strong, who went on to defeat Paul's old buddy Pat in a one-sided final.

"How are you, Brian?" I uninterestingly asked Brian before we started our two minute warm-up. I knew it would be exactly two minutes as Brian is Mr. Rulebook and that is the maximum time a warm-up period is meant to last.

"Ready to go Des?" Brian remarked after 118 seconds.

"No," retorted I but with a smile on my face. Win this game and I would sort at least one of the other two. I was more than capable of beating all three but I clearly also had the capacity to lose to all three clowns.

You know the drill, Des. Brian is about 120 years old so speed would be my weapon. I had one last long look at the red side of my bat hoping big dog was ready to bark.

"You are going to feck this up today," started Bad Des.

"Shut up" I utter. Brian put his hand up ready to complain to the umpire, Mark the bleeding octopus McAlister, before I said, "Sorry Brain, just thinking to myself."

First two sets and big dog was floating about, I ground out a 2-0 lead. Slow, fast, slow, slow, super loop, and smash. Sometimes it works and sometimes it doesn't. Suddenly I was 6-4 up in the third and I was serving. Time to think about Dave Butler next. A 3-0 victory will help if there is a countback in the group.

Seven minutes later it was 2-2 in sets and Brian F…ing Finn, the defender, was smacking me about the place. Where is 'coach of the year'? I was thinking. And then I was 9-2 down and almost down and out.

"Time out!" I scream. You are allowed to take a two-minute time out to gather your thoughts and discuss tactics with your coach. My two coaches were nowhere to be seen as they were also attempting to qualify out of their normally 'easier' groups.

Dirty tactics time I think. Mark was a million miles away and I knew he would not have timed the time out. Brian was ready to go at the exact time. Good man Brian, I was not. I was in the corner facing the wrong way talking to you know who. Yes, Bad Des had become my coach. As I slowly moved back into place Brian tapped his watch. The break had been 2 minutes and 47 seconds.

"Mark, Brian Finn wants to know what time it is."

"Ah." Mark suddenly knew what I had been up to and started laughing. Brian was not a happy camper. Just as he was about to serve Bad Des suggested *"Just go over there and hit him full on in the short and curlies."*

With the serve launched, I had no option but to catch the ball and say, "I wasn't ready."

Brian just glared at me as I stood there and smiled. During the next six points I launched a full-scale counter offensive. Big loop, whack, big loop, whack, big loop, whack. It was high-risk stuff but before long it was 9-8 and Finn was a dead man walking. If I could win his next serve and then my two serves, Brian would be mine. I glared at him with a stupid smile on my face. The Octopus was finally awake and loving it. I knew he would serve long down my backhand, so I was already there and ready when he sent it. Up goes the ball, contact, long down my backhand, I was there but holy fuck the ball went straight down the line and I couldn't get anywhere near it. Our neutral umpire McAlister was in stitches laughing as he turned the score board to 10-8 in Brian's favour. It was so bad that even I started laughing. But I still had my two serves.

I will serve it hard down his backhand, he will paw it back and big dog will dispatch it down his forehand. Then repeat and it will be deuce in the fifth and nervous nelly time. What a contact, the ball flew down Finn's backhand, but what is this? The 120-year old was flying around that side of the table and whacked the ball down my forehand. It was all over. Lost to Brian F…ing Finn 11-8 in the fifth. I wanted to kill someone but as Brian approached with that big, big, big stupid grin on his face, I grabbed his hand and talked to him for almost two minutes.

Next up was Dave Butler and before I knew it, I was 2-1 and 8-1 down having to call another time out.

Unfortunately, Mr. Brian Finn was umpire so 1 minute and 57 seconds later the battle recommenced. I did absolutely nothing because the big dog was nothing but a little pup that wanted to go home. Somehow, I fought the whole way back but still lost 11-9 in the fourth set. I was out and my international career was over.

Before long, the octopus and I were at it again. Although

out, my nemesis still needed sorting. I go up 2 sets to nil but against Mark this means nothing and nothing is precisely what I end up with. Another 3-2 defeat and I have the wooden spoon. Last in my group just merely a few weeks after losing in a final. *"Plonker, Dessie is a plonker"* started my dear friend Bad Des.

Out cold with coffee to buy on the way home, I wandered over to see what had been happening to the lads. Anthony White had taken Dave Pemberton to a closely fought fifth set but ultimately to no avail, and with that, Omagh's representation was over for the day.
Paul, the Donegal Slapper, had made it out of his group but had failed to make the last eight. No fun on the way home I was thinking, but what about the Chinese loving Derry Head Mr. Sean McAnaney.

I sat down beside Paul, muscling in on the coaching position, as Sean started his quarter-final against our favourite Connacht head, Mr. Kieran Burke. Kieran should have too much for our Sean, but you never know. 12-10, 12-10 to Mr. Burke before 'coach of the year' went to work.
Over the next twenty minutes, I watched as Sean played some of the best table tennis I have ever seen him playing. Winning the next three games 11-7, 11-9, and 11-8. It was hard to work out who had the bigger grin, Sean, or Paul 'coach of the year' Gallagher. With my dismal performance from earlier beginning to fade, I laughed to myself as I knew I was going to be the butt of all jokes on the way home.

Next up was my Croatian knight in shining armour, Mr. Branislav Jakovetic (Branko). Sean started by defending but before long was blocking in at the table with his pimples (Sean might be the only pimples player that will not end up in hell) and counter-attacking. Both men were on top for periods but eventually, Sean won a fascinating battle and sure enough our Croatian friend was hugging Sean and wishing him all the best for the final. It was great to see two very popular lads (58 + 62-year-old lads) enjoying their sport. Sean has done loads of work promoting table tennis and continues to use his Chinese connections to help anyone and everyone.

Unfortunately, the final was a relatively straight forward affair with Pat McCloughlan running out with a 3-0 victory.

"How come you never win any semi-finals?" I asked Paul.

"What do you mean?" Paul replied

"The last two finals have had representation from the north west bus in them but never you."

Paul smiled and walked away realising what Des Flanagan's only line of attack was going to be especially round the time of handing over coffees.

Without much enthusiasm I started working out the new league table, trying to see how much trouble I was in. Apart from Celtic FC, my other two football teams were always in trouble, namely Omagh Town FC and Birmingham City FC. Looking at league tables rarely cheers me up.

Position	Name	Tournaments Played	Total Points
1	Kevin Mackey	4	670
2	Pat McCloughan	3	580
3	Nebojsa Gobric	4	400
4	Mark McAlister	4	380
5	Paul Gallagher	4	360
6	Phillip Shaw	4	340
7	Kieran Burke	3	330
8	Dave Pemberton	4	320
11	Branislav Jakovotic	3	270
13	Des Flanagan	3	270

Slim and slimmer would now be my chances of playing international table tennis in Dublin in September 2020.

It Takes Balls…

12 Journey Home From Munster Open

Sean, Sean, Super Sean, was the theme for the early miles of our journey back to the North and back to civilization. Everyone was delighted that all Sean's hard work had paid off. "Where are we stopping for coffee and magnums, that Des will be paying for after his super performance," shouted somebody.

"Ok, ok lads. I suggest that we stop at both Applegreens on the way home and I will buy everything."

"Good man Des."

"Yes, this car journey will be sponsored by Des Flanagan Investment Solutions, the greatest financial advisor on James Street Omagh."

I asked Sean, "Do you ever think any of these other clowns will ever win a semi-final like we have done in the last two tournaments?"

"When is the last time you played international table tennis Desmond?" butted in Paul. "Remember myself, Mark, and Dave Pender, were the team two years ago."

"That was only because it was held in Guernsey and none of the big lads wanted to go," I countered.

"Des, have you got the football scores yet on that ancient thing you call a smart phone?" gently asked Anthony, not fully aware that all return journeys start with abuse flying everywhere.

"No premiership, it is FA cup 3rd round day. Do any of you clowns remember how big this used to be before money wrecked English football?"

"Can we just get the scores without the commentary please Des?"

"What would be the fun in that?"

"How do you lads put up with Des when I'm not in the car?" interrupted Anthony.

"We don't listen to a word he says," said the two lads in unison.

"Birmingham City beat Blackburn Rovers 2-1."

"Who cares?" suggested Paul.

"Fulham stuffed the Villa 2-1."

"Who cares?" groaned everyone.

Anthony asked me, "How did United do?"

"Which United?" I taunted.

"Manchester you fool."

"Wolves stuffed them 0-0."

Paul innocently asked how anybody could be stuffed nil-nil, he's not the greatest football fan in the world.

"Leicester City 2-0 Wigan Athletic. Manchester City 4-1 Portsmouth"

I pointed out that the Barcelona Derby ended 2-2 to which Sean replied "I didn't know there were two teams in Barcelona."

"Espanyol are deemed Franco's team in Barcelona and the Barcelona fans hate them. In fact, very few Barcelona fans would even go to Espanyol's ground."

"Who is Frank?" asked Paul.

"General Franco, Spanish Civil War 1936-39. Do you know anything Paul other than how to lose quarter-finals and semi-finals?"

"I know who Franco is, I just thought you said Frank," retorted Paul.

At this stage, everyone was wondering how we got from Saturday's football scores to the Spanish Civil War.

I remained quiet for about two minutes deciding whether to go down the political route or the road of stupidity. After the stories about Bloody Sunday and the Omagh Bomb earlier in the day, I decided to do stupid, something that comes very naturally to me. As I was in my rightful position upfront, I had some level of control. Noticing that Sean still had that awful big grin on his face and was likely to be in contact with his girlfriend in China, I decided to go hard. Turning off the radio I uttered the following.

"The protestant and unionist communities have got the whole GAA thing wrong."

"Explain," asked Anthony.

Paul and Sean groaned because they knew I was about to launch into one of my monologues.

"Now lads I need you to concentrate on this one."

"Do we have any choice?" asked Sean.

"When was the last time one of you clowns was at a Gaelic club match?" Without pausing for a breath, I continued. "How long into the match before the first punch up, ten minutes?"

"About that," confirmed Anthony.

"Surely the unionist community should be encouraging all these nationalists/republicans beating the heads off each other. It should be a spectator sport for them. They would love it. They could meet their heroes during the week and help provoke the fights." Total silence in the car and some shaking of heads.

"Now taking matters up a level. The unionist community could form supporters' clubs and attend en masse. Even better and this is where this gets interesting, we could combine the various Orange marching bands into pre and post-match entertainment."

"Have you been drinking again?" asked Paul.

"Think about it lads. If you knew that there was going to be an orange marching band down the away end could you imagine the attendance."

"What about those clubs with no local marching band?" inquired Sean, realising that this conversation could go anywhere.

"This is where my plan becomes brilliant, Playoffs or band offs.

"What are you ranting on about Des?" said Paul.

"Any club without access to a local Orange band could apply for a cross-community grant to promote Orange band competitions in their area, with the winners being that GAA club's representatives for the following season."

I realised that my plan would take a while, with the main problem being that all the bands would want to represent the same club, and what club was that? The Rangers, Crossmaglen Rangers.

"The marching competition could be held round Cardinal O' Fiaich Square in Crossmaglen. Could you imagine the crowds lads? However, we would possibly not want to schedule this competition to clash with an old firm match between Rangers and Celtic. Imagine the tension if Rangers got another one of those dodgy penalties or offside goals. What do you think lads?"

Absolute silence.

"Ok then, what if I reorganised the GAA into a national

athletics organisation?”

"Des, two more minutes and that is it," ruled Paul turning the radio back on.

Turning the radio off I continued. "Every GAA club promotes all forms of Athletics. Be it running, hurdles, long jump, javelin, shot put, etc. And they get a grant depending on how many people from it qualify for county games, then provincial titles, then national titles. We have the same population as New Zealand but look at the amount of Olympic medals that they get compared to us."

"Who exactly are us Desmond?" asked Sean.

"The island of Ireland you clown."

"Coffee time," shouted Paul, indicating to turn left off the M1. "Thank God" was the verdict within the car.

Twenty minutes later we were back in the car heading for Applegreen number 2, but Des had been relegated to the backseat alongside Sean and he was not happy about it. This time Anthony took over in the hot seat and so he diverted the conversation in his favour. "Do any of you lads play chess?"

"Here we go," shouted I.

"Shut up," shouted Paul and Sean simultaneously.

For the next half an hour I was totally caged in and ignored, despite the fact that I am a professional interrupter. World champion of that title being a certain Cormac O'Hare from Milford, Armagh, and record goal scorer for Oslo 81 according to himself anyway.

"So, you are telling me that you can take up to three days to make a move playing online chess?" Sean asked Anthony incredulously.

I shouted, "and you think I'm boring."

"Shut up Des," came a tirade of all the voices in the car.

"You move at that pace as well playing table tennis Anthony!"

103

"Shut up Des"

As the journey continued pub quizzing was brought to the top of the agenda, an agenda that I had lost total control over. As I am totally useless at quizzes, I turned my attention to Sean who was stuck in the back with me. No matter what Sean and I attempted the two lovebirds in the front would continue to ignore us.

"Show us her photograph," I pleaded to Sean. Surprisingly, he turned his phone in my direction to unveil the famous Chinese girlfriend.

"You are doing well for yourself there Sean," I suggested. That stupid big grin reappeared. "I suppose you have told her that you are the greatest table tennis player in Ireland."

"She already knows that Des," laughed Sean.

Friendly fire continued in the back for the next twenty minutes whilst the love-in continued upfront. Paul was amazed by Anthony's knowledge on all things musical.

"How do you know everything about music?"

Just then I worked out how to counterattack regarding the front. For the next 15 minutes, I listened as Anthony correctly named every artist and song on Pauls random songlist. Finally, he shouted out Iris De Ment. He had been struggling for a while on that one. Again Paul stated, "That is amazing Anthony."

"Bullshit" I exclaimed from the back. "Paul do you not know what that clown Anthony White has been up to since he seized control of my seat." Anthony started smiling because he knew where I was headed. "Have you ever heard of that app Shazam? Anthony has it on his phone. Have you not noticed how he has been moving his phone close to the radio for the last half an hour?" Sean started laughing and Anthony smiled.

"You Omagh boys are all the same, you always have an

angle. Are you taught it in school?"

I replied with "Remember Paul, Anthony is the Vice Principal of my old school."

The rest of the journey home flew with complete stupidity the whole way. "Told you Anthony would greatly increase the IQ level in this car." I told the other two.

"He has certainly doubled the average IQ of the people from Omagh" was the overall consensus as we all parked at the Crevenagh Road park and ride. A long long day had ended with joy in our hearts. Thank God for those car journeys.

It Takes Balls…

13 Journey To Glenburn Open

I didn't want to play table tennis today. Yesterday I was in my car between appointments when the news came through of the death of Mr. Seamus Mallon. All I could think about was Seamus' daughter, granddaughter, and son-in-law, all of whom are known to me. I would be going to the wake but currently wasn't sure whether to go today, Saturday, or tomorrow morning, as the funeral arrangements had been announced for Monday. When in doubt about these types of things I always head straight to my beautiful wife Edel. Edel is a calmer person than me and is a great sounding board. She is also very logical and we both discussed the options. I could be of little help today or probably tomorrow. But I must say farewell to someone whom I no longer related to as a client but as a friend. Over the previous few years, I had visited Seamus twice a year in his house in Markethill with every visit following the same pattern. Five minutes work and up to two hours discussing current affairs, history, and Irish politics. It must be the only house that I have ever been in where I have done the vast majority of listening. Since the announcement of his death only hours before, I found myself constantly referring to his excellent book 'A Shared Home Place'.

Because I was due to do the driving, Edel convinced me to play the Glenburn Open and go to the wake the next morning. Also, she didn't want me moping about the house all day. I sent a text to the son in law Mark, which helped to calm me down.

As I drove through the archway at James Street by the Sinn Fein offices, I bumped into one of the Polish families that now occupy most of the apartments beside my office. Mietek and Penata were up early that morning I was thinking, before realising that Mietek wanted to talk. As I have no Polish and he has no English these conversations are always interesting. He simply wanted to give me another dozen or so eggs. Obviously, I had no need for eggs that day but I could always throw one at Brian Finn if I had to play him. After a bit more pointing and shrugging of the shoulders I opened the door of my office and put the eggs in the fridge.

I had given all four polish families Marks and Spencer's vouchers for Christmas. Daria from Kwvidzyn had written all the Christmas cards in Polish for me and I thought this was a master plan as I now had four sets of security people for my office. When they all purchased me individual gifts for Christmas in return, my master plan had turned to genius. Full office security for the entire year for about ten quid.

As a history buff I would be reasonably well versed in Polish history and to distract myself from the terrible news I had finally watched the movie '302 squadron' which is all about the heroic Polish airmen of World War 2 and their pivotal role in the Battle of Britain. Fortunately, all the other Polish neighbours have excellent English so various political discussions have taken place. Wonderful people and great addition to our society. But how would they vote in a future border poll? This is a question for another time as Paul and Sean had just turned up 32 seconds late.

With me driving, the boys very quickly settled. They knew how highly I thought of Seamus Mallon so they simply asked when I was going to the wake and asked to pass on their regards. They also knew that I would have a full-blown conversation regarding Seamus when the time was right.

As we drove up by the CBS school, I thought it was time for another Phil McCusker story, simply to lighten the mood.

"Did I ever tell you the story about me and McCusker and our A level English exam?"

"No, but I have a feeling you are going to," teased Sean gently, knowing that it would lift my spirits.

"Well as I was doing History, Economic History, and English, and Phil was only doing Biology and English, I thought I would delegate the reading of the English books to Phil."

"What do you mean?" smiled Paul sitting beside me in the front.

"Very simply, I had no time to read the likes of 'Little Dorrit' by Charles Dickens or 'Othello' by a Mr. William Shakespeare. However, I might have time to read proper notes if I could get someone intelligent to write them. Fortunately, the aforementioned McCusker was a highly intelligent 18-year-old (apart from that mad notion to go to Brussels) and also an extremely neat hand writer. Thus he was dispatched to read the various books and I would read his notes and nothing else.

On that famous A level results morning I was standing beside Phil when he announced his two C's. Of course, with me being the organised one I got an A in History and a C in the other two subjects. We got the same

C in English. To this day if I am ever in Phil's company and a fifth alcoholic beverage is consumed, I always start into Phil about how if his notes had been any better, I would have gotten a better A level in my English.

The last time I had uttered this had been in early December in the Wicklow Arms bar in Bilbao Northern Spain. I had asked the owner, Michael, from Wicklow, if he would give me and Phil a free pint each if he thought my story was worthy. He did not give us a pint for this one so I tortured him for the next couple of hours with story after story until he relented, closed his bar, and joined the Bilbao two for a couple of hours giving us a locals view of his beloved new home town. We are fans and will be back to annoy Michael further.

It was only a few miles later when the tonic of a McCusker story had worn off and my mind was heading into darker territory. The death of my father almost exactly a year before that of Seamus Mallon's, 22nd of January 2019 to be precise. My relationship with my father has always been clouded by one thing. Unfortunately, whisky was the problem here. My father was always a storyteller and a fisherman and would normally combine the two. Growing up in a house with two other fishing-obsessed males, it was hard to get a look in. As a very shy teenager, I had to sit and listen for hour after hour. Fishermen can talk some amount of rubbish, but Flanagan fishermen are international class. You can divide these stories into four distinct categories; totally true stories made up one percent of the total, mainly true made up forty-nine percent, partly true made up forty percent, and almost completely false made up ten percent. The male species of the Flanagans concentrate on the latter and adore the complete lies category. You also have to add in the lateness of the hour and the consumption of alcohol to the equation, and then there would be no need for a lie detector at all. The bloody thing would break. Interrupting a male Flanagan with 'you have already told me that before' is a pointless exercise as it only encourages them. As my father was a physics teacher, he knew the percentages. The final factor is age. As you get older you migrate towards the almost completely lies category. This is where the fun is. Who is going to tell an 86 year old man that he is lying. Anyhow, they will simply let on that they cannot hear.

Regarding this effort of a book either 80% of every story I tell is completely true, or else 80% of the content of every story is true. I'll let you figure that out.

I always enjoyed listening to all the stories but particularly the fact that storytelling is an art form and how you can play with a crowd. My father may have finished telling stories, but he would continue with the whiskey. He was never violent but verbal abuse would quickly appear on the scene. Strangely, he would turn his attention to those that he had taught who had became successful or very successful. I never understood this aspect of his character and in later years would confront him by saying I had recorded what he had said. Looking back now it is obvious that he would never remember what he had been ranting about.

Shortly after I met Edel in 1990 Dad announced that he had given up the drink and would be marrying Gunn Amelin, a Swedish woman. True to his word, he never drank again. I believe that this added years to his life, years that he seemed to fully enjoy. I always wonder what my relationship with my father would have been like without the alcohol.

What was troubling me as we drove to Belfast was mainly the last nine months of my father's life. He had walked into a door and broke his hip. The length of time spent in Altnagelvin and Omagh hospitals changed the man and damaged his confidence and independence. There were plenty of instances where Gunn and my father had fallen out with various carers. It was obvious to the entire family that these people were doing their very best. They were excellent but Gunn was simply not coping with all the visitors. She is an extremely private person and this marriage was definitely a case of opposites attracting. A nastier side of my father's character also appeared where he was quick to criticize those around him.

I had been deeply troubled because I knew I was simply looking into my own future and recognising character traits that I also possess. Not nice to see your own weaknesses in front of you.

Shortly after Gunn left to go back to Sweden, we as a family had to quickly organise a nursing home for my father. Fortunately, the manager of the care home selected happened to be a client of mine, and I warned her what my father may be like on difficult days. Within two months my father was dead, but I was questioning my own role in his later years. Had I visited him enough? No. Had I listened to his stories enough? No. Had I been patient with him? Certainly not. But why? This was the question that was troubling me. His death had also brought back other more recent incidents within the family circle.

Two of my sisters had lost children in the last decade. Aggie had lost her daughter Ciara to suicide and Deirdre had lost her Tracey. Had I been a good enough uncle to either? God only knows but again it all troubled me. Yes, I had organised and completed a family cycle form Mizen to Malin for charity but was this enough? I was either overthinking or beating myself up too much.

I now have a theory that my father, my older brother Seamus, and myself, are all so similar that it is uncanny. All three of us like to be telling stories, be centre stage, and have no concept of the skill of listening. Was this the reason for a recent outburst or all-out attack on my brother? God knows, but the death of Seamus Mallon had clearly upset me, and I hoped that some good may eventually come out of it. Only time would tell. Now it was time for a table tennis tournament, but I would have been happier to be sitting in a certain house in Markethill. My mood was not good, despite every effort from my two amigos in the car.

It Takes Balls…

14 Glenburn Open 25/01/20

After the satnav successfully found 6 Glensharragh Gardens in Belfast it was yet again time for battle. I really needed some form of a soft draw in the over 40's to get my day started. I felt absolutely wrecked and I hadn't even hit a ball yet.

Kevin Mackey and Anne Marie Nugent were my opening opponents and Kevin soon dispatched a very under strength Desmond. One set down and behind in the second set to Anne Marie, McAlister butted in from the sides trying to wind me up. If the octopus had remained silent, I would probably have lost this match as well. I managed to raise my game sufficiently to scrape by into the knockouts. Although I believe that I can beat most people on my day, I have the capacity to lose to virtually anybody if my concentration isn't there.

Against the number one seed in knockouts, Daryl was simply too good for me, so I was quickly out. Glancing round the hall, or halls as the Glenburn Open is a split venue, the North West bus would be providing nobody for the day's quarterfinals. Time to sit back and enjoy the later stages of the over 40's knockout tournament. No disappointment here as we were about to watch the game of the season in the final between best of buddies Daryl Strong and 'fast' Phil Wallace.

The opening four sets were shared and 'fast' Phil raced away in the fifth to lead 9-4. Daryl is not one to give away a title so he called time out. This broke Phil's momentum allowing Daryl to edge back into the game which seemed to get inside Phil's head. Phil had three match points and to me was too passive, maybe hoping for a mistake. Daryl made no such mistake finally winning by 13-11 in the fifth. Did Daryl win this or did Phil lose it? A little bit of both. I think you must beat Daryl with all guns blazing, guns that I do not seem to possess.

Wriggle room gone I would need a bit of luck in today's over 50s draw to bring myself back into contention for the Ireland B team. Dave Pemberton, Dave Gibbons, and Bryan Morrison. I had a 100 percent record against Gibbons and Morrison and managed to maintain it. The match against Dave Pemberton would be a repeat of the Ulster Open semi-final, and I knew that my former international teammate would be out for revenge. To call this a classic would be simply wrong, it appeared that both of us wanted to lose this as mistakes were the order of the day. Being two sets up to one, I again froze, so into the fifth we went. Fortunately, Paul 'coach of the year' Gallagher was at hand having just qualified as the winner of his group.

"You are snatching at everything…Seventy percent loop then big dog!"

Bang, bang, and the game was over. For once I had actually listened to Paul. Might have to buy him a magnum on the way home again I thought.

After qualifying out of my group I watched as Paul Gallagher beat Dave Butler to reach the quarter-finals. Next up was Branko vs Sean. Sean again beat Branko, thus winning his group. Unfortunately, he lost to Dave Pemberton in the last 16 wherby he duly sacked me as his coach. Paul 'coach of the year' Gallagher had not been available as he was playing. Before long I watched Paul beat local hero Norman Nabney in the quarter-finals. Then it dawned on me who I was playing next. Yes, Brian F…ing Finn.

For some strange reason, I felt quietly confident. Winning my group meant I avoided the big two and because it was knockout out time it would be win or bust especially regarding any lingering hopes of an international table tennis comeback. It also helped that I liked the hall as it wasn't too far removed from my favourite table in St Columba's Hall in Omagh. There was no need for tactics. Like myself keep it simple Des. All-out attack from start to finish and if you get ahead of Brian just finish him off, unlike the last time giving up a two-set lead.

Behind the whole way in the first, I scraped through to win the opening set. Slightly ahead through the second and finished going away from him. This time Des, all-out attack to kill him with speed and power, remember he is an old man. It was 9-4 to me and Brian F…ing Finn called a time out. I smiled at him and tapped my imaginary watch making sure he wasn't going to pull a Des Flanagan on this thing. He won the next point making it my time to serve. A big long one deep into the backhand then big dog was the plan. There was no need for coach of the year this time. Plan works and I had five match points. For once big dog delivers a brutal slap down the forehand. A full-blown Tyrone slap which is of a higher quality than a simple Donegal Slap. Game over.

As I headed towards Brian F…ing Finn to shake hands he shook my hand but paused. "Des not only do I want to congratulate you on today's performance but I personally want to thank you for saying what you did after I beat you the last day out." For a good two minutes he recounted my total sportsmanship in defeat. How I had stated that the best man had won, the best man had deserved to win, and how his tactics were brilliant.

"Can I now say to you exactly what your final words to me were?" he asked. "Good luck to you in the rest of the tournament and I am already looking forward to our next match."

At this very point, Brian F…ing Finn became known as simply Brian Finn, sportsman, and buddy. New York sure did seem like a long time ago.

Next up for Flan the Man was home favourite Wee Willie Cherry who happens to be quite a big lad actually. Since my return to vets table tennis, I had not yet beaten Wee Willie. In our junior days, I had a one hundred percent record against him as we were frequently battling each other for a place on the Ulster team. We would eventually be on the same Ulster team, alongside Richard McWilliams and Brian Orr, that finally won back the inter provincial crown after a gap of almost ten years. Today, however, I needed to ask Wee Willie about our past. In my memory, I had used the sectarian card to motivate myself to make sure that I beat Willie and made that Ulster team. In my head table tennis was a Protestant sport in Ulster, whereas in reality, it was a sport where the participants were predominantly Protestant. There is a huge difference between those two positions, and I was keen to get Wee Willie's impressions. But first I needed to end that losing streak.

If I beat Wee Willie I would be back in contention. The first set was crazy, net after net followed by edge after edge and Willie was blowing a gasket. He somehow won the second set against the run of play, but I bounced back and slaughtered him 11-9 in the third. It was obviously going to be my day and after exchanging blows early on I started getting on top. Another edge and Wee Willie was about to crack. 8-5 up leading two sets to one it was 'hasta la vista' to Wee Willie and a place in today's semi-final. I shouted 'hasta la vista' to myself and went to work on Wee Willie.

… Several minutes later I trudged over and shook Wee Willie's hand and wished him all the best for the rest of the tournament. Yes, I snatched defeat form the jaws of victory and felt like a complete idiot

"Hasta la vista, hasta la vista, and one last time for good effect, hasta la vista," taunted Bad Des. *"You are the greatest plonker ever to have played a game of table tennis,"* he continued.

I didn't know whether to cry or cry so I cried internally. I had gone for it, but the edges were now just missing but at least I went for it, I tried to console myself.

Later I walked over and plonked myself down beside the victor Wee Willie Cherry. "You were lucky there Willie."

"Nonsense Des, how many nets and edges did you get? It must have been 10-2 in your favour."

On reflection, Wee Willie had a point. Over the next few minutes, we discussed all things junior Ulster and Irish table tennis from back in the late 70's early 80's and we both smiled about things we had gotten up to. Especially me and Alan 'tank' McCormick in Bradford.

"Do you remember me and you stuffing Brian Orr and John Fall in the final of the Irish Championship junior boys doubles?" Willie asked.

I was stunned into silence. "Please repeat that."

"Yes me and you have a joint Irish national title together. You were winding John Fall up and he fell for it hook line and sinker. Brian Orr got annoyed as you talked non-stop during the game and used that stupid anti loop rubber to great effect. Especially the stamping of your foot every time you served, that really got to him. I think the umpire called you for gamesmanship a couple of times, but you were having a ball. You hit with the anti-loop and the ball popped up and I banged it home."

"So, I made you look good," I teased, still in a state of shock.

"Brian and John were furious with you by the end."

"Nothing changed there I see. I wonder was that why John Fall screamed 'Scooby Scooby-Doo', a couple of years ago in the Ulster vets after finally beating me on my 55th birthday," I wondered.

"Probably."

This was an entire chapter of my life that I had forgotten up until then.

With that bombshell Wee Willie was off to play his semi-final against Kevin Mackey, a game he was to win. In the other semi-final, Paul blew another chance against Pat McCloughan.

In the final I watched Pat beat Willie but by now he was the second person to receive a name change. Any person henceforth that is a national champion alongside Flan the Man will be known as Big. Thus, Big Willie was born and from now on I could say my Big Willie, for the first time in my life. Strange day indeed. Brian Finn loses the F and Wee Willie becomes Big Willie and I had become an Irish National title holder. God help the boys on the way home now. I would certainly buy coffee and Magnums, that is what national champions should do.

How does someone play table tennis alongside someone at Liverpool University for three years and not remember their name and how in the hell does someone not remember that they are a national champion?

"God help us all Desmond."

Now it was time to work out the overall standings for the journey home.

Position	Player	Tournaments Played	Ranking Points
1	Pat McCloughan	4	780
2	Kevin Mackey	5	780
3	Paul Gallagher	5	560
4	Mark McAlister	5	450
5	Dave Pemberton	5	410
6	Nebojsa Gabric	4	400

Selected Others:

7	Sean McAnaney	4	390
8	Branislaw Jakovetic	4	360
8	Des Flanagan	4	360

I was now back in the game.

It Takes Balls…

15 Journey Home From Glenburn Open

Thank God for table tennis. It had proved to be the perfect diversion from the darker side of life that Seamus Mallon's death had provoked. I was hoping to keep things light on our journey back to Omagh before the lads headed for Letterkenny and Derry respectively.

"If my calculations are correct, Paul is heading for the A team, and Sean and myself still have a chance of forcing our way on to the B team."

"I will need to get to another final," responded Sean.

"Sean, tell Paul what playing in a final is like," I suggested.

"Both of you lads got stuffed when you reached a final," replied Paul now sitting in the back for once.

This type of banter continues until the coffee and Magnums had been purchased by me at the Applegreen at the start of the motorway.

"Did I ever tell you clowns about how me and my Big Willie won a national title together back in 1980 or 81?"

"No, but I have a feeling that you are going to tell us all

about it Des," teased Sean.

"Indeed, I was so good that I even made Big Willie look good." For the next ten or twenty minutes I gave the boys a point by point description of an event that I had no memory or recollection of. But why would that ever stop a male Flanagan from telling a story? If there is an element of truth in the story it's classed as a true story.

Nearing the hour I switched over to Today FM to get the day's football scores. Again, no premiership football but rather Scottish Premiership and the fourth round of the F.A cup dominated affairs. Birmingham city drew 0-0 away to Coventry City at their own pitch at St Andrews. It took a bit of explaining to the lads that Coventry city had leased St Andrews for one season to play all of their home matches.

"Lads, did I ever tell you the story about Keelan and myself getting on Match of the Day?"

"Now this one must be complete lies," suggested Paul.

"For once, one hundred percent true."

"Go on Des, as we have no option but to hear it," replied Sean.

"Back in season 2010-11 Birmingham City F.C were sponsored by F&C Asset Management, and they invited me and a guest to this match. I was doing a lot of business via F&C then. Anyhow, about five minutes after arriving at the pre-dinner meal I was approached by a young lady to see if my son would like to lead out both teams at the start of the match. Quick as a flash, which is not like me, I replied as follows; My son Keelan would love to lead out both teams, but as he is of a such nervous disposition, his father will have to be standing beside him. At this point, I could feel Keelan kicking me under the table. The young lady said she would have to check with her boss. Needless to say just prior to the match the two likely lads were leading both teams out at St Andrews."

"Where does Match of the Day come into this Des," asked Paul.

"Patience Donegal Slapper."

"Continue Des," Paul suggested.

"10:15 that night back at the Jury's Hotel, I turn on BBC 1 just before Match of the Day. Due to bad weather, only two games had been played that day. Five minutes later as Gary Lineker introduced the first match, there were two lads from Omagh right in front of me on the telly leading out the teams. Boy was I a proud Dad watching myself and Keelan on Match of the Day."

After another couple of my stories, I decided enough was enough. Paul was bored and Sean is only interested in football if Derry City or Liverpool are playing. I again bored the lads ranting on about how Celtic were going to win nine in a row this year and dominate Scottish football into the near future. Little did I know that the very next day Rangers would lose to bottom club Heart of Midlothian 2-1 and go on a losing streak. Celtic 3-0 Ross County put us top of the league where we would stay for the rest of the season.

Switching to the BBC N.Ireland news there was plenty of talk about Seamus Mallon and the role that he played in the Good Friday Agreement. When the news ended, I told the lads everything that I knew about Seamus and his politics and simply what an impressive man he was. I told them about all my visits and our various political discussions. In short Seamus Mallon was possibly the most impressive person I have ever met and for someone like me who was so interested in current affairs, Irish politics, and especially the way forward, it had proved to be a Godsend. For once the lads were interested in what I had to say.

As I dropped the lads off, both of them thanked me for the day and wished me all the best for Sunday and Seamus Mallon's wake.

16 Journey To Wake

As I headed out of the house just before 10 o'clock, I quickly realised that this would be the second wake that I would be going to in this particular house. Back in October 2016, Gertrude Mallon had passed away after a long silent battle with dementia. Seamus had ended his long political career to do the honourable thing and look after the love of his life. When the news came through about Gertrude, I decided to head straight to Markethill. Fortunately, Edel had accompanied me on that particular trip. I still believe Seamus was in a state of shock by the time we arrived. Edel and I were warmly welcomed, and we sat around with a few other early visitors whilst Seamus recounted some of their time together. In a strange way, it was a very tranquil hour or so. Seamus had been particularly kind to Edel, whom he had never met before. On future visits, he would always ask about her. On reflection, it had been the right decision to bring Edel. She was providing me support whilst I was trying to provide some support to Seamus and his family.

By October 2016 Seamus was almost like an uncle to me. He was of the same generation as my father and his brothers Patsy from Gortin, Seamus from Carrickmore, and Father Brian who had been a priest in America. The other connection was that apart from Father Brian, the rest of them had been teachers, most of them through the '50s '60s, and early years of the troubles. Additionally, and more importantly, they were educationalists. A percentage of my clients were taught by my father and everyone thought highly of him.

This time around, Edel knew that this was my journey and something I very much needed to do myself. After getting the coffee in and smiling that only one coffee needed to be purchased rather than the usual three, I pointed the car in the direction of Markethill. It was time to review everything that had happened between myself and Seamus.

It all started back in April 2011 when I was out doing an annual review for Seamus's son in law Mark and his daughter Orla. At the end of our meeting which was much shorter than usual, Mark stated that his father-in-law wanted to have a word about possibly setting up something for their daughter. He also stated that I would know him when he walks through the door. I was in a state of pure panic as I am a complete control freak. What is Orla's maiden name? Come on Des, come on think. About five seconds before his entrance the name Mallon popped into my head and I instinctively knew that Seamus Mallon was about to walk into the room.

He did not walk but strode into the room, nearly crushed my hand, and sat down opposite me, dominating the room. He was a big man with a big presence and I instantly thought of the comment by someone who's name is also not coming to me, "Seamus Mallon is the only man that can intimidate you with the words 'good morning'."

The next ten minutes were the only ten minutes of Mr. Mallon's time with me that I didn't enjoy. I was back in the principal's office having to listen. He set down his terms and conditions, what he wanted and how much he was willing to invest. Towards the end of this monologue, I remembered that I was the professional financial advisor and maybe it was time to speak. I was no longer actually listening to Seamus but thinking of my counter-attack. Instead of a professional story regarding the best way of doing what he was looking for, I came up with diversionary tactics.

"My wife Edel has a theory about the Irish."

"Go on," replied Seamus.

"They are not in the slightest bit friendly but rather we are bloody nosey. Let me give you an example. We see two tourists in a bar drinking their half-pints and people approach them and the tourists think we are friendly. What is actually happening is that we are so nosey that we need to find out if they are German, Dutch, or French. It is our nosey-ness that is misinterpreted as friendliness. In my case, it will normally be to settle a bet in my favour." A certain Mr. McCusker will no longer play this game with me.

I continued. "Yes Seamus, I have taken all that on board, and what day next week are you available for a meeting in Markethill?" I had just ended his role as the school principal by launching my counterattack. With our next meeting agreed I saw that twinkle in his eye. He knew what I was up to. I wanted to see his house, see his book collection, and see where this big man had operated from throughout his political career. I would use every dirty tactic possible to get Seamus Mallon on board as a client. I would reintroduce the wheelbarrow approach to financial services. What is the wheelbarrow approach? I hear you ask. Go to someone's house and put a little bit in the bottom of your wheelbarrow and head off. Return again a few months later when that person is officially a client and put some more in the wheelbarrow. Within a couple of years, you will have taken over the entire garden and you will start issuing instructions. Like myself, simple but brilliant.

However, the next few days were not straight forward as I was nervous for the first time in years. I did not want to mess this up. For the next few days, I actually did substantial research and was prepared. I also knew that the first five minutes would be vital, so I planned those down to the last detail.

I was brought into a much, much smaller room than I had expected. Through the garage, I was brought. Does he do this with` all the big wigs? I asked myself. I was directed to sit at a right angle to Seamus while he finished a phone call. Immediately my eyes were off round the book collection. Various Irish history books that I had read, 'Long Walk to Freedom' by Nelson Mandela, I could start there. However, it was two photographs that really caught my attention. One was of some lad called Bill Clinton and the other was a Polish guy called Karol Jozef Wojtyla otherwise known as Pope John Paul II.

"Where shall we start Mr. Flanagan?" interrupted Mr. Mallon. Indeed, my name is Des I thought, and with that, I threw out my carefully worked strategy and started.

"Before we start, I need to know the answers to the following two questions," I asked. "Who is the most impressive person you have ever met in person, and what was the most interesting phone call you have ever taken?" I would show the schoolteacher that the pupil was now in charge, or so I had hoped.

Seamus smiled and replied, "The most impressive person I ever met is actually relatively straightforward, Karol Jozef Wojtyla."

"Pope John Paul the second," I interrupted trying to impress.

He growled at me so I quickly shut up.

"Yes, John Paul II. I met him for ten minutes before we went together for a private mass said by a young Polish priest. I was with my friend Billy (I wondered if this Billy also supported Rangers). Afterwards, we talked for a period. He was wonderful and you could just sense God in the room and in the man, what a presence. After this chat, I approached Billy and asked him why he had received communion and him not a catholic, to which he replied, 'Just in case you bastards are right and God is a catholic'."

We both burst out laughing. It was just like my dad telling his stories.

As I am writing this actual chapter, I have just received an acceptance of my Facebook friend request of that very Billy, yet another Billy had come into my life. Is Seamus messing with us from above?

Reading Seamus Mallon's book, I realise that he tells that story quite differently, claiming that Billy's response was instead "It is my God too you know." Seems like Seamus could change a story to introduce a stronger punch line, just like someone else I know.

Impressed, I turned my attention to the phone call question. "It was a few days after the signing of the Good Friday Agreement and I received what I thought was a prank call from the local radio station, I was not going to fall for that. However, I quickly realised that one of my heroes was actually phoning me to congratulate us all on the Good Friday Agreement." Seamus paused at this point for effect.

"Who was it for God's sake?" I asked.

"Nelson Mandela.

"<u>The</u> Nelson Mandela."

"Yep."

We continued like this for the next ten minutes before I remembered why I was there.

"Where do I sign Des?" and like that, I was Des, no longer

Mr Flanagan. I was in. I attempted to go through the 1064 pages of stuff the regulator wanted me to go through, but no, Seamus simply wanted to give me a cheque and sign the forms.

Seamus asked me, "How much do you get out of this Des?"

"Not enough" was my initial answer. I told him that I was waiving all initial fees because of the work that he and others had done. I also personally thanked him because the peace process had allowed me the freedom to raise my family in my beloved Omagh. He again nearly crushed my hand and thanked me for thanking him.

"I do get paid an ongoing fee for looking after the investment," I informed him.

"So you will be back Des?

"Whether you like it or not, yes." I had the wheelbarrow to fill. With that, we ended our second ever meeting and with that, I retired asking the two questions of who is the most impressive person you have ever met, and what is the most interesting phone call you have ever had? Who could ever beat Pope John Paul the second and Nelson Mandela?

Normally I conduct an annual review of my clients' finances and for this, I am paid an ongoing fee. With enough clients, the annual fee covers all the office costs and leaves me with a sufficient income to raise a family. Eventually, you get to the point that you're not under any pressure for new business and, because you are not under pressure, the appointments become more fun. I tend to go all over the place going to and from meetings with new clients and if I think they are interesting or if they can tell a story they will be quickly accepted. It also allowed me to do some pro bono work for deserving causes or people who have fallen on hard times who simply need a helping hand, especially with reorganising debts. This can be the most rewarding part of the job. As regards to Mr Mallon I simply wanted more time in his company. Instead of an annual review he would get the privilege of a review every six months.

These six-monthly reviews would quickly form a pattern. If the stock market was booming, I would take all the credit and spend twenty minutes talking work and as long as possible talking politics, history, and current affairs. If the stock market was going through the floor it would be everybody's fault but mine, five minutes work, and as long as possible on politics. On the rare occasion that Seamus declined an appointment his request would be totally ignored because something urgently needed done. I would turn up and our routine would continue. Over the years the wheelbarrow got fuller and fuller and I looked forward to my visits with my new 'favourite uncle'. In fact, himself and Uncle Seamus (The good Seamus) were quite similar. Both could tell a story and were passionate about their communities. I believe Seamus Flanagan turned down an OBE from the queen.

When asked if he would receive the honour my uncle supposedly responded, "As I am from Carrickmore and would like to continue living there, no I will politely decline, but if there are any grants going…"

So twice a year for nine years Seamus Mallon and I would meet up and various subjects would be discussed. The subject matter would frequently be decided by current affairs within the north. Throughout this time period, it quickly became obvious that our views were very similar. It was also bleeding obvious that myself, Orla, and Mark, were all benefiting greatly from the work of Seamus and his colleagues who had worked so hard to build the peace process. A solicitor, a dentist, and a financial advisor all trying their best for their clients and patients. We were the new breed of professionals coming out of the Catholic community but why were we being antagonised by the harder element of unionism? Just as the Ulster Unionist Party had mistaken the SDLP as their enemy the DUP were now doing the same to the softer nationalist community. The amount of times I agreed with Seamus over this point. If I had become the public relations officer of the DUP the tone would be different.

History will view the last ten years as an opportunity lost by that party. There was a growing band of nationalists that were quite happy with the status quo that the Good Friday Agreement had granted, now we wanted to build our own futures for ourselves and our children. Brexit would change things and change things utterly. I am of the firm opinion that the DUP have changed the course of history by their approach to Brexit. I believe that a large part of the party thought that David Cameron's referendum would never result in a 'no' vote. Thus, they decided to take the 'high ground' and argue in favour of leaving the EU. We all know the election result now, but the actual result may not be known for years. What it did do was to change nationalism. Again, the DUP had fired people into the hands of Sinn Fein. Those of us who have absolutely no time for the hard-left policies and who hate the violent history of that party have decisions to make. We need to convince unionists that we want the same thing. We want to build the land of many names into a land of one purpose: prosperity, and a just society for all.

After Gertrude's death, I used our six-monthly visit to initially suggest and later beg Seamus to write his story down. I would also suggest this to both Orla and Mark at every opportunity. I am now fully aware that this pressure was building from many sources. I feared that without Gertrude to mind, Seamus might fade without a purpose. I forcefully argued that soft nationalist, nationalist, unionist, republican and loyalist voices all needed to hear his story. I believe that it was a southern commentator that finally pushed him over the line.

The commentator asked, "are Sinn Fein rewriting history?"

I simply urge that everyone should read his book. It should be on every school curriculum and if it becomes an English A level book than even a young me would read it. His hatred of violence and contempt for the republican movement jumps out at you. At Gertrude's wake, he was anxious as he wanted no member of Sinn Fein near the place.

Some of his more interesting stories and tales from his past were told when I enquired about certain individuals known personally to Seamus but only on the news to me. Here are a couple of examples:

"Tell us about Enoch Powell."

Off Seamus went into a world I knew nothing about. "Enoch had questioned a Wilfred Owen quotation during my maiden speech and sent me off to the library for further research." These two characters clearly made an intellectual bond initially and I felt a personal bond forming as time went on.

"Tell us about John Hume."

These stories were endless and very favourable. Although Seamus feared for the consequences of bringing Sinn Fein in from the cold, he knew that it had to be done. He feared that the middle ground in the north would be squeezed but I argued that the middle ground is where all the victories are finally won.

Most interesting of all was his response to one of my final questions. "How will history judge David Trimble?"

"You tell me what you think first," he replied.

I had and still do believe David Trimble will be highly thought of by historians. I personally think highly of him.

Without him what would the peace process have been like? Just like the SDLP, David Trimble would eventually be squeezed out, but hopefully, there will be a return. Unionism needs David Trimble back, we all need David Trimble back. What the hell is he doing in England?

Seamus Mallon thought so highly of David Trimble himself and was so thankful of his role in the peace process. I was so glad to hear that David Trimble had made it to Seamus Mallon's death bed.

My final thoughts as I approached Markethill for the wake were the stories Seamus told me of asking Trimble technical questions in Westminster and him having to answer them in a technical manner using up his speaking time, all with Seamus just sitting there grinning. Good times indeed.

As I pulled my car in beside the incline heading up to his house, I was so relieved to notice that the big ugly UVF sign had been removed from the telephone pole. The UVF also need to read Seamus's book, they might learn something from it. Seamus Mallon should not have a UVF poster outside his house, instead, the people of Markethill should have a statue of him up.

Interestingly after his book was published, on our final meeting on the 11th September 2019, he had informed me of the number of unionist neighbours that had contacted him wanting to meet him in private. Many had called to say thanks in person, but a number had called to express their shock at some of its content. Many had believed that state collusion was simply a Sinn Fein propaganda tool. They never for one second actually believed it had ever happened. With that, we had said our goodbyes and now I was seconds away from the hardest visit of my life.

17 The Wake

As I gingerly headed through the front door, I was reminded that this was only the second time I had entered the house through the front door, only previously for Gertrude's wake. I could see Orla over to the left, but she had not noticed me. Mark was quick to greet me and thank me for coming. He escorted me into the room on the right and there in the corner was what I had come to see but never wanted to see. I stood silently beside one of my heroes and said a quiet prayer. As I am one of those bad Catholics who don't know much about Catholicism I sometimes struggle in these moments. I feel more spiritual than a connection to one specific religion. I am strong of the opinion that all of this did not just appear. If you lie on a beach with one grain of sand representing earth and the universe represented by the beach, you quickly realise how insignificant we all are. I felt that small and useless at this particular moment. I rejoined Mark in one of the other rooms whilst he thanked people who had come from all over Ireland. I watched for ten or fifteen minutes as Mark expertly controlled the room trying to shield Orla the best he could.

I suddenly had the urge to say my final farewell to Seamus. Fortunately, there was nobody else in the room when I entered. I walked slowly over and bent down and whispered something into his ear. As I headed out to find Orla, I could feel tears welling up in my eyes. I turned to see Seamus Mallon one last time, although he was there it was a different figure that I saw. Seamus had obviously agreed with what I had said because I was now looking at a certain Gerard Desmond Francis Flanagan, my Dad. I was no longer welling up but instead, I let the tears come. I knew where I had to go next. I found Orla and without speaking simply squeezed her hand and said my goodbyes. Orla acknowledged my gesture and with a final shaking of hands with Mark, I was off and heading straight for my offices at James Street in Omagh. It was such a peaceful journey back to Omagh via Armagh with a nod to Cormac O'Hare, past Aughnacloy with a nod to an old buddy Plunket Donnelly, and finally round the back of my Office.

I was staring straight at the last thing I had asked for from my father. It was his Queen's University Certificate.

'It is hereby certified that Gerard Desmond Francis Flanagan was admitted to the Degree of Bachelor of Science by the Queen's University of Belfast on the 10th day of July 1951.'

For years it had sat on the wall beside my high-quality third-class honours degree from Liverpool University but I had never noticed what was now jumping out at me. It was not the course, nor the university, but simply the date of graduation. The 10th day of July 1951.

Why had I never noticed it before and why had I never asked my father about it? He had obviously entered Queens University in 1948 directly benefiting from the most progressive bit of legislation ever passed by the unionist dominated Stormont. The Education Act of 1947.

It was the Northern Irish version of the Butler Act in England and Wales, and the Education Act for Scotland. It allowed all children aged over 11 to access free secondary education as well as introducing university grants, medical treatment, transport, stationery, and free milk for all students. In the next 10 years, the number of students in secondary education would double. Through this act, a greater amount of Catholic children could gain higher education, including political activists such as John Hume, Seamus Mallon, and Austin Currie.

The importance of the Education Act was huge for my father, my family, and my entire generation. Why had I never asked my father about his university days? What was the political landscape like between 1948 and 1951? How had things been for my uncles and their generation?

I clearly had benefitted personally from the act. Dad went to university in 1948, myself in 1981, and my daughter Anna had started her medicine degree at Glasgow University in 2017. My son Keelan is due to head off this year and Junior whenever he decides. I was also thinking of all my cousins and all my mates from the Omagh CBS. Most of them had thrived at University. The Education Act of 1947 was more important than we could have imagined. Progressive Unionism at its best.

Good memories of my father started flooding back. All his stories, even the completely stupid ones. Little things like the books I would buy for him for Christmas. I always bought him three history books when I was home from University. They would always be the three books I wanted to read myself. My Da would finish them all off over Christmas and I would bring them back to University with me. 'A Bridge Too Far' was obviously one of them.

There was one last place I now had to visit and fortunately it was on the way home.

Ten minutes later I was standing directly in front of my parents' grave.

'In loving memory of Susan Flanagan died 13th January 1984 aged 53 years. Her beloved husband Gerard Desmond Francis (Dessie) died 22nd January 2019 aged 88 years.'

My mum was speaking directly to me again. I had to stop blaming dad for my mum's death. She had died from a brain haemorrhage and ever since I had blamed my Dad's drinking for her death. Finally, I said sorry to my dad.

As I stood there silently, I started to reflect on other instances when my mum had stepped in and sorted me out. Along with Fred, she had got me sorted and motivated to pass my law degree. Just as importantly she had stopped my gambling before it really started.

On my 18th birthday in February 1981, just prior to our epic Belgium trip, mum had given me cash to buy some clothes or a new table tennis tracksuit. Being fond of numbers and knowing how to beat the system, I had invested the money in the offices of Barney Curley Bookmakers, Castle Street Omagh.

On returning home I had tried to sneak into the house.

"Show us what you bought."

I knew how hard she had worked for the money I had gambled away. I simply could not lie to my mum, so I told her everything. She gave me the biggest hug and simply asked me to stop. The shame and disappointment on her face was enough. One bet every five years since must have saved me so much money over the years. Thanks, Mum.

As I drove out of Greenhill Cemetery and turned left towards home I reflected on the day. Mum, Dad, and Seamus Mallon were of one generation, and I had a lot to thank them for.

18 Journey To Connacht Open

Again, the routine. Three pairs of socks, not so new table tennis shoes with go-fast stripes down the side, spare pair of shoes, two pairs of shorts, three shirts to make me look fit, a tracksuit, two hand towels, two bats and a water pistol. No wait, I should replace that with two boxes of Celebrations sweets, one for my new buddy Brian Finn, and a bigger one for my fellow national junior boys doubles champion Big Willie Cherry.

Heading off into town, I was in good form. I was reflecting back on Seamus Mallon's wake and the immediate positives that had entered my life. Thankful that I got to know Seamus, resolved my differences with my father, and the realisation that I needed to start loving myself before healing other relationships. I could feel fun in the air, or was that mischief?

Passing the Orange Hall I noticed that there was no Union Jack flying. I have no understanding of what the rules are anymore. I must admit that I have absolutely no issue with the Union Jack flying above orange halls. Some of my best results have been inside them.

Paul was only turning left by the Sinn Fein offices before I started into him. "What were you clowns in the south doing last week in your general election? You had a modern leader, Leo Varadkar, and the Fine Gael party that rebuilt the southern economy brick by brick and that's how you reward him."

Democracy is a wonderful thing but sometimes I worry about the people. For the next ten minutes, I spouted off about the election.

"Explain to me Paul how this is going to work? Fianna Fail have 38 seats (including the Ceann Comhairle), Sinn Fein have 37 seats and the real leaders have 35 seats. Civil War politics will finally have to end in the south lads."

Paul replied, "Are you saying that you are a Blueshirt Des, a northern Fine Gael head?"

"Indeed, I am. The SDLP want to join forces with Fianna Fail and that is not progress. If we can ever vote on an all-island basis the nationalist vote in the north would split along Fianna Fail and Fine Gael lines. Imagine for a second we had a 32 county election. Before that, the parties would have to realign. Sinn Fein and Fianna Fail would have to merge, the social democrats and the Labour party would need to change, the sole unionist party would be returned with the largest number of seats and for a minority government they would form a coalition with my party, Fine Gael."

"What time in the morning is it?" muttered Sean. "It is too early for this Des."

"Have you taken your happy pills or something?" asked Paul

I continued at Paul, "I see the old double standards in the south have emerged again."

"What do you mean… and is it left here?"

"Yes, left by the school," I directed him. "Immediate right then immediate left. Just like the last ten times you clampit."

"Do you want to drive then?" he sharply responded.

"No, my knee is still sore."

Paul got us back on track. "What were you saying there about the south's double standards?"

"Basically, Fianna Fail, Fine Gael, and the southern elite are saying that it is okay for Sinn Fein to share power in the North. But no way are they getting into government in the south. Balls, balls, and more balls. I am no fan of Sinn Fein but by God are they passionate and hyper-organised on the ground. They put their policies down on paper and argue the point to death. Any time I have engaged with any Sinn Feiner out the back, they know their stuff. In fact, I thoroughly enjoy bumping into them. I had a great five-minute chat with Martina Anderson the MEP out the back of my office on the evening of the Brexit referendum. Our five-minute chat must have lasted 90 minutes. If you ever get Barry McElduff off the phone, he can also chat."

"What ever happened to Barry?" asked our southern representative.

"We will not go there again. He got himself in a wee bit of bother, but I actually believe that he didn't know the significance of what he was doing. He had to go because he is supposed to be representing all the people."

"Can we change the subject please?" demanded Paul.

"Do you want a McCusker story or one of my dad's stories then?"

"Jesus, we have never heard any of your dad's stories," replied Paul

"Don't encourage him," warned Sean.

"Do you want an interview story or one about teaching in Nigeria?"

Paul decided "Give us a story about teaching in Nigeria."

"Ok, we will start with the interview stories," I replied, totally ignoring Paul.

"Just after he graduated, my Da went to Oxford University for a job interview."

"Where?" Paul seemed quite shocked.

"Oxford University in England, remember us Flanagan's are super intelligent."

"God help us all; this is going to be a long day," muttered Sean.

"Anyhow my Da entered the room and the dean of the faculty was sitting behind his desk with one foot on the table reading the Financial Times. 'Good morning' my father started but was ignored. By the way, never ignore a Flanagan, it is dangerous. My father sat there for almost five minutes without the dean uttering a word. My father realised that it was some form of a test so he remained silent.

"A silent Flanagan, I don't believe that," said Sean.

"What happened next?" Paul asked politely.

"The Dean eventually stated, 'if you want this position, Mr. Flanagan, get my attention.' With that my Da sprung into action and got out his box of matches and lit three of them simultaneously. He duly lit the Financial Times which was still being held firmly in front of the Dean's body. 'Holy God Mr. Flanagan, what are you doing?'. My Dad replied with 'Getting your attention Gobshite.'

There was silence in the room for another two minutes while the dean made his decision. 'On reflection Mr. Flanagan you might be a bit too smart for this institution'. My father said 'you are probably right. In fact, my entire family would be too smart for this institution. Before I go where do I pick up my expenses?'

My Da had a masterplan. Get as many interviews as possible Wednesday, Thursday, Friday, and then head up to Accrington to visit my future mum where she was nursing at the time. Come home and turn down all the job offers."

"Why would he turn down the job offers?" asked Paul.

"He could not afford to take the jobs."

"What do you mean?" Sean was slowly warming to the story.

"He was getting expenses for the train journeys and the boat journeys from every potential employer because of the quality of his degree. All paid in cash, no questions asked."

Before the boys got an opportunity to speak, I was straight into the second interview story.

Back in 1983, my Da was reading the local Mayo paper and saw a job offer for Westport House, Head Gardener wanted, salary negotiable. That was a job for him so over he went and phoned the number in the advertisement. I overheard him saying that he had no time to fill out an application form and somehow wrangled an interview for the following Tuesday. I had a fair idea what he was up to.

Tuesday morning came and there was no way I was going to miss this. Before my dad knew, I was in the car and off to Westport House with him to meet Lord Altamont, the owner of Westport House. Surprisingly, my dad seemed quite nervous. After finding our way to the west wing we finally entered the reception area for the interview. The young girl on duty could only have been about 18 at most, my father started blethering away at her. If he was not doing that he was pacing up and down the hallway. Finally, we noticed Lord Altamont crossing the lawn and my dad went straight over to the receptionist just before his arrival.

"What do you call the old bollocks when he comes in?" smiled Des Flanagan Senior.

"Well I call him daddy." With that, I was on the floor laughing as his lordship walked in.

"What is going on here?" he exclaimed.

I pointed straight at my father and said, "You better

ask him."

Off the two likely lads went and I waited over two hours before they reappeared. In this period about six other people turned up for the interview. I also failed totally to arrange to meet the beautiful young secretary for a drink. As they re-entered the room the two lads shook each other's hands.

Lord Altamont said, "See you again Dessie."

To which my father answered loudly, "this lot are wasting their time then."

The lord smiled widely, and I instantly knew what was, or had been, going on. My father had never wanted the job but had simply wanted a personalised private tour of Westport House, and who better to get it from than the owner.

"How come your Da's stories are better than yours?" asked Sean. Totally ignoring the Derry head, I proceeded straight to Nigeria, St Patrick's School in Calabar to be precise.

The first day back to school in year two of his two-year stay, my Da was up front in the classroom in one of the new prefab buildings. This school was for the elite of Nigerian society and my dad was loving being the only white person in a 200-mile radius. After about 15 minutes the noise levels started rising from next door. As Flanagan's do not like getting interrupted or annoyed, he went next door and let a roar out of him. This worked temporarily but had to be repeated about half an hour later, this time a lot louder. Another half an hour later Des Flanagan senior cracked and he knew the answer. For the first of only two times in his teaching career, Mr. Flanagan resorted to violence. He found the tallest lad and clipped him round the back of the ear. Absolute total success. There was complete and utter silence until lunch break.

At lunch, my Da marched off to the canteen happy with his morning's work. Entering the canteen, he was waved over to join the school principal who was with someone vaguely similar to Da.

"Mr. Flanagan welcome back to Nigeria for your second year. I want to introduce you to our new teacher, a former past pupil."

With that my father finally recognised the well-dressed tall teacher, "I think I may have already introduced myself to him."

Over lunch my Da explained what had happened that morning, finally realising why the class had been so quiet. The only white man in a 200-mile radius had hit the teacher. Apparently, my Da and this new junior teacher became the best of buddies over the course of 1953 in west Africa.

"That's the first funny story you have ever told," shouted Sean from the front with a stupid grin on his face.

At this very point, we were driving past Markethill very close to Seamus Mallon's home and I gave him a little nod of thanks. Finally, I could reflect back at my dad's stories and start to laugh again.

"What about a McCusker story? Do you want to hear about his greatest moment, the moment he became leader of the entire Republic of Ireland football team's supporters?" I asked the two lads.

"Not really but I have a feeling we are going to." Sean smiled at Paul who also had a stupid grin on his face. "Is this a short one Des?"

"Certainly not but it is pure genius."

It was 1988, the 12th of June 1988 to be precise. The entire country was celebrating its greatest ever sporting achievement. We had just stuffed England 1-nil with a Ray Houghton special. 'Who put the ball in the English net, Rayo, Rayo' was being sung everywhere. Emerging that day

147

from the attendance of 51,373 at the Neckarstadium Stuttgart was a certain Mr Phillip McCusker, Cannondale, Omagh. The next time Mr McCusker would be in this stadium I would be with him and Celtic would be qualifying for their next round of the UEFA cup. By then it would be known as the Mercedes Benz stadium. Progress not.

A few hours later Phil was heading back to his hostel on a bus full of Republic of Ireland supporters. He was virtually asleep when he took one last peep out of his window in the dying seconds of the 12th day of June 1988. He couldn't believe his eyes. He immediately jumped into action. Straight up to tell the bemused bus driver his plan. Temporarily taking overall command of all ROI supporters, he gave his detailed instructions.

"Only full colours please and all flags to the ready."

Operation Undertake was launched. Commander McCusker was to receive various lifetime awards for this manoeuvre. The driver flashed the warning lights and slowed the bus down. The bus behind started overtaking as planned. 5...4...3...2...1...GO. All curtains were pulled apart, all windows opened, all flags out. With virtually everybody hanging out the side of the bus ignoring all health and safety rules, Commander McCusker launched his greatest attack against the English forces.

"Who put the ball in the English net, Rayo, Rayo," reverberated from the supporters' bus.

The attack was on the official bus of the now defeated English national football team. The next two minutes were the greatest of a young McCusker's life. The dog's abuse was of the highest quality and it was relentless. Public information announcement. None of the following were physically injured in this operation; Peter Shilton, Chris Wood, Tony Adams, Viv Anderson, Tony Dorigo, Kenny Samson, Peter Reid, Brian Robson, Trevor Steven, Chris

Wadde, Dave Watson, Neil Webb, Peter Beardsley, and Gary Lineker.

The last of the England squad to close their curtains was a certain Mark Hateley with a middle finger raised. McCusker and Hateley would cross paths again when the England player joined Rangers.

"Even I watched that match," stated Paul.

"No more stories Des," replied Sean.

"No more politics either," responded Paul as we continued. For the rest of the journey, I switched off with a feeling of contentment washing over me already looking forward to doing battle on the table again.

It Takes Balls…

19 Connacht Open 15/02/20

The only way to describe the Over 40's tournament is to call it a lucky dip with a bit of everything in it. It started so well. The group was myself, Dave Pemberton, Pierre Bouhey, and my nemesis Mark '10 bats' McAlister, or the octopus as I was now calling him because of his rather long arms. I would qualify if I could beat Mark. I had gained revenge for my two earlier Irish ranking defeats by beating him in the final of two grand prix events within the Greystone League and stuffed him in a league match at home as well. Unfortunately, he had won the Division One championship title with me winning the overall series. Thus we stood 3-3 year to date and about 15-15 in the last three years. But I loved playing him, he would rarely use his preferred pimples when playing me because he knew I would probably win.

But before playing Mark I had to beat Dave Pemberton, whom I had by now beaten twice this year. I raced into a 2-nil lead and was playing well. I somehow managed to lose the next three games 11-9 and thus the showdown with Mark would decide runner up. The stupid clown decided to use pimples and duly got stuffed. Thus, I had qualified, but nobody had told Pierre whom I had never lost to. My one hundred percent record soon went as I lost on the dreaded countback. In fact, Mark had messed about before beating Pierre 3-2, otherwise he would have qualified. So what, life is good and I would sort out the world in the over 50's.

Sean was having a stinker, but Paul Gallagher reached the quarter-finals. The highlight of the over 40's involved my coaching qualities when I took a young Rodney McKirgan under my wing. This is the very Rodney McKirgan that had single-handedly wrecked my birthday exactly seven days earlier.

The final tournament to decide the positions in the Ulster Interpro's was held seven days earlier in the Church of Ireland hall in Newmills, my favourite, and now luckiest venue. In the final group of four, myself, 10 bats, the Donegal Slapper, and captain McKirgan meant that the winner would be joining Daryl Strong and fast Phil Wallace on the Ulster team. I beat the Donegal Slapper 3-0 and Mark 3-1 (actually this meant that I was 4-3 up for the season) and only had to beat Rodney to claim my rightful place on the Ulster over 40's interpro team, on my 57th birthday. Rodney lost to Mark 3-2 so even if I lost 3-1 I would qualify. In addition, I had stuffed Rodney 3-0 at his place in a league match and that match had not been close. Also, because it was my birthday, I had brought Junior along to take photographs. What could go wrong?

Rodney McKirgan did not know it was my birthday and he kicked me all over the place, utterly hammering me 11-4, 11-3, and 11-4. I was furious, but this only lasted for 2 minutes and 17 seconds. No Ulster team, so everything depended on Irish qualification.

Rodney lost his first game to Dave Pemberton but I

called him over to coach him, or in reality, I just lectured him.

"Last week you stuffed me with an all-out attacking game and now you are just farting about. Attack, attack, attack." Fifteen minutes later the recently appointed captain of Dungannon Golf Club was congratulating me

"You owe me a round of golf, and I will stuff you at that as well," I told him.

"Do you ever give up Des?" Rodney replied.

"No surrender!" came my surprising answer.

Needless to say, Rodney McKirgan did not fully listen to my instructions but fought all the way to lose 3-2 against Kevin Mackey in the quarters. Not my fault though.

I can't remember who I played in the group stages of the over 50's but I know that I stuffed them all and was into a quarter-final with guess who? Mark 'The Octopus' McAlister for our eighth battle of the year. In the meantime, Sean bombed out of his group more or less destroying his chances of qualification for the Irish Team, but Paul 'Mr. Consistent' was to reach yet another quarter-final but fail at that hurdle. I really, really needed to beat Mark, my season depended on it. Would he use pimples or go live?

"Show me your bat, Mr. McAlister."

"Say please."

"Live I see. Too scared to use pimples?"

Thus, the battle had started without a point being played. Start fast, Des. Attack, attack, and dominate.

After winning the toss, I opted to receive, which meant I would be serving at the end of the inevitable fifth game. Also, it gives a great opportunity to impose yourself on the game by attacking both of your opponent's first serves. I believed that he would go very deep and very wide to my backhand, or straight down the line. Watch his wrist Des, that will give it away.

"Ready Des?"

"Ready and willing Marcus, time for battle," I responded with a big grin on my face.

Don't watch the ball, watch his wrist and nothing else. Up went the first ball. Watch, watch, watch. He was going down my backhand and I was off running. With the entire table exposed, he went very deep and very wide and very spinny, but somehow, I managed to get there and launch the big dog straight down the line.

"Is that the best you have got?" I shouted loudly.

"It's talkative Des today then," smiled Mark.

I had and still have no concept of whether Mark loves playing me or hates playing me. But I intended to have fun.

Serve number 2. If I won this I would not only be two-nil up but I would already be inside his head. I reckon only Mr. P Harrington from golf has more going on in his head than 10 bats McAllister. I was just going to guess this one and go very early and see what happens. This time the big dog was waiting, and I looped the ball straight past Mark. I milked the entire situation by holding both of my hands aloft. Mark was not happy but that was the purpose.

For the first two sets, I judged every one of Mark's serves and jumped into a fully deserved two-set lead. To Mark, being 2-0 down means nothing. If I ever go to his funeral, I will wait around until everyone is gone just in case he attempts a stupid comeback. Talking of comebacks, he scraped the third set and dominated the fourth leading 10-7. At this point he forced a mistake out of me, I easily popped the ball up for him and he casually knocked it over the endzone. Big mistake Mark. I sensed that he thought it was all over. It was then that the big Cookstown fool served one down the line but off the table. Flan the Man now led the octopus 5-3 for the season, but more importantly, I had a semi-final to win, assured that I must now have been in the top six and heading for my international comeback after 40 long barren years. Apparently, Mark let go of his bat as it flew by my coaching staff, which had doubled in size to include both coach of the year Paul and assistant coach Sean.

About five minutes later I wandered over towards Mark who still seemed to be muttering to himself.

"How can you lose to that idiot not once but twice in one day?"

Unable to resist and with Bad Des' full approval I responded, "You will need a third bat to play me next season Mark."

He looked at me and didn't know whether to laugh or cry "Go away."

And with that I was off to face one of the big two, Pat McCloughan, also formerly of Liverpool University but with a very impressive economics degree, unlike my third-class honours masterpiece. Ten minutes later the battle commenced. I knew I was playing well. Before long I had taken my first ever set off Pat and I was serving to go two sets up. I had closely watched his game against Big Willie in Glenburn, the same Big Willie that hadn't shown up to today's tournament. In that game, I spotted something that I believed I could use to beat Pat. Unfortunately, he won the titanic second set and pulled away from me to win 3-1. He went on to win the tournament. Did I actually believe that I could beat him? Maybe. I vowed that next year I would fully believe.

Shortly after we all headed for Paul's car, I was in a very content and almost peaceful mood. It was time for a bit of mental maths from the greatest financial advisor on James Street, Omagh, County Tyrone. Up Tyrone I say.

League table live update.

Position	player	Tournaments played	Ranking points
1	Pat McCloughan	5	980
2	Kevin Mackey	6	940
3	Paul Gallagher	6	560
4	Mark McAlister	6	540
5	Dave Pemberton	6	520
6	Des Flanagan	5	470
7	Branko	5	450
8	Phil Shaw	5	440
8	Sean McAnaney	5	440
10	Dave Gibbons	6	420

One more performance and I would be there. Also, the last tournament is the national championships with additional points available. I was wondering if Branko was eligible. Had he qualified under residency rules yet? Also, the national championships bring out a few of the better players who may not have played too many tournaments and would thus be floaters, namely my Big Willie. Anyhow, I would have taken this table that morning I woke up in New York. I was in a good place heading for the car, Paul was nearly qualified and Sean lived to fight another day. One more good performance and my forty-year wait would be over. Roll on the national championships.

It Takes Balls…

20 Journey Home From Connacht Open

As we headed for home, I knew that being the car player of the day would exclude me from having to buy either the coffees or the Magnums. Just prior to bringing up the subject, Sean must have been reading my mind because he volunteered to buy. As I was fiddling with my phone trying to get the football scores the BBC news came on. The topic was Coronavirus and the fact that the 9th person to contract it in the UK had been confirmed. Paul flicked between the various stations to see if there had been any cases in Ireland; north, south, east, or west. None had been reported.

Our onboard China correspondent Sean quickly brought us up to date with what was happening there. By the 15th of February China had just over 900 confirmed deaths and over 400,000 confirmed cases. A general discussion ensued but without anybody being able to add much. In simple terms, we had no idea what it all meant or how it would affect us. I mentioned that the stock market is a good indicator and was remaining quite close to all-time records. However, stock markets have a habit of overcorrection and I feared for the workload and the stress that this would cause.

"Sean, Liverpool won 1-0 away to Norwich City and Southampton lost at home to Burnley 2-1," I mentioned.

"How did Omagh Town do Des?" asked Sean.

"Still unbeaten this year," I almost snapped back. But as I was now becoming the new and improved Des Flanagan, I quietly conferred this information. The boys just laughed.

I asked the lads, "Do you want a Phil McCusker story, a classic from my Da, or Donegal related big brother story?"

"God we are hearing them all today Des," responded Sean.

"Is the Donegal story a funny one?" asked the Donegal slapper.

"Of Course."

"In the famous summer of 1992, the year Donegal won the first of their two All-Ireland titles in Gaelic football, I had just passed my driving test. I was working for a few months with my brother Seamus selling aerial photographs."

"What's an aerial photograph?" asked the ill-informed Chief Finance Officer for some American company.

I responded, "a photograph taken from a plane or a helicopter normally of a house, business, small business, or a small village. They can be used for promotional purposes. Today you would probably use a drone."

Anyhow, we started outside Muff and continued selling our way up via Moville and into Rathmullan. After a couple of weeks learning on the job, staying locally, and having a couple of beers per night, Seamus produced the best photograph of a large house that I had ever seen. He showed it to me expecting the obvious reply which I duly gave him. "Why would he want an aerial photograph of his house when he could take one in the helicopter that was clearly visible in the photograph?"

Seamus replied with "Tomorrow I will show you an expert in action." My brother like my dad was a real storyteller, but a young Desmond had no idea how he was going to manage this feat.

After confirming that the helicopter and large 4x4 were present at the property when the door opened Seamus named the owner instantly and handed him a few samples. I later discovered that Seamus had done his research in a very typical Irish manner, in the pub the night before over a couple of pints. No need for doctor google. After a couple of minutes of banter, the owner asked Seamus his name. He then asked Seamus the following bleeding obvious question.

"Seamus, give me one good reason why I should buy that photograph off you when you can clearly see a helicopter in the photo, that I could clearly use to take the same photo?"

"If I can give you one good reason will you buy the photograph off me?"

"Yes," said the increasingly frustrated owner.

"How the bleeding hell are you going to get your own helicopter in the photo?" And with that Seamus proceeded to walk straight past the owner and into his house adding "I also have about twenty photographs of those factories you own in town if you are interested."

I duly followed my big brother into the kitchen and listened as he talked big numbers and took a very large sum of cash as a deposit for multiple sales."

"You are all bandits in your household," stated Paul.

"Never trust a Flanagan," continued Sean.

Up until our pitstop to allow Sean to purchase the refreshments I told tale after tale regarding the summer of 92. The only real summer I had with my big brother Seamus. Even I laughed at some of the stupid tricks he used. As the summer progressed, sales increased because Donegal went all the way to winning the Sam Maguire. The reason for the increased sales was the increasing number of banners and Donegal flags going up all over the county. By All Ireland weekend it was time for the match, or more exactly time for me to meet Paul Murphy, 'the Dub', to watch the match. Seamus suggested we both go but I said no. He was to stay and work. I would go to the match or watch it with Paul Murphy and pray for a Donegal win, and big brother would fly all day and take pictures of people's houses on the day Donegal won their All Ireland. Donegal won, Seamus, flew, and I took money from Paul Murphy at odds of 5-2. Nice piece of work if you can get it.

My final lesson of many that summer from my brother came a few days later after I had received maximum price for an aerial photo of a small cottage in rural Donegal.

"We are going back in cub," stated Seamus.

I listened as Seamus asked the family how many sons and daughters had come home for the match and how many children were living abroad. Two came home and three were in America. At that very moment, one of the sons came in and before long every member of the family had a photograph of their home on the very day that history had been made. Next trick was to get the son to name the actual households in the list of photographs held by Seamus. He sent him ahead to warm them up. The greatest training course I ever went on and I got paid very well.

"Both your Dad's stories and you brother's are better than yours," said Paul, pulling into the Applegreen.

"Large coffee, americano, no sugar, and the biggest dearest magnum you can find Sean," said I.

"Yes Sir."

I said virtually nothing for the rest of the journey but started reflecting on another part of my life, namely my love life with the movie 'Sliding Doors' constantly popping into my head. The 'what ifs' of my life have always interested me and because Edel was to play the biggest part of all, I was drifting off into a happy place.

Don't panic, my love life will not take too long. Before meeting Edel I somehow managed to fall in love three times even though I never even kissed one of them. Let me explain how my life was to change forever and for the better. Keep in mind my earlier trip to Brussels and that word 'fate'. The following stories all occurred during my time working for Dunnes Stores in the south of Ireland.

1986 Elizabeth Letterkenny

I approached her whilst she was helping her mother in her promotions work within the store. She was a dentistry student and highly focused on her career. We spent two weeks on the Greek island of Crete together, unfortunately, she broke up with me on the plane on the way over. We still had a wonderful totally unplanned holiday. Elizabeth was my first proper girlfriend and I was twenty-three years old. A very slow leaner was our Des.

1987 Ciara Tierney Terryland Galway

Ciara was the sweetest thing and I spent most of my working time on Friday evenings and Saturdays with her in the fruit and veg department. I did exactly what my brother had done and never asked her out because it was against the rules. Didn't stop Paul and Shelly Murphy though. After I transferred, I learned that Ciara had been outside McSwigan's on my birthday but was too shy to enter. Sliding doors moment here. What if…

1988 Niamh Ballina

This one lasted longer than any of the rest. It ultimately was more painful because I had started to plan ahead in my little head. Also, I lost a couple of her friends as well, especially her right-hand woman at the time, Lesley. A

Christmas cake incident was my downfall here and unfortunately, I was guilty.

In table tennis terms I had a good season with Elizabeth but was beaten hands down. I failed to enter the competition regarding Ciara, and I was shown the Red card in regard to Niamh. In my defence, I was trying to do the right thing but did it completely the wrong way. Sorry, everyone.

18/03/91 O'Donoughue's Bar Merrion Row Dublin

I was sitting beside the ladies toilet by accident when I first noticed her. An attractive talkative young lady in a larger group of slightly louder ladies. I was halfway down my second pint of Guinness with no real notion of where I was going to stay because I had just fallen out with Paul and Shelly Murphy whom I was supposed to be staying with. Turns out the argument was about nothing. They had famously gotten married on the day that the Republic of Ireland played Italy in the Quarter Finals of the World Cup. An interesting day indeed.

How to approach this young lady was quickly becoming an issue. I could have just walked over there but there was six of them. It had the look of a Venus flytrap about it. Also, there was at least one Tipperary accent and even I was not that brave.

Before I could come up with another plan she was on the move and heading straight towards the ladies toilet. When she finally emerged, I was accidentally on purpose in her way.

"Hello, there are two girls in here that I fancy, and you are one of them."

"Get me a pint of Guinness and show me the opposition," she replied.

Nervously, I started into a bunch of unrelated stories

that I thought were funny, somehow finishing with our trip to Brussels in 1981.

She said "I heard that story in here last week from some lad based in London, although he told it somewhat differently. I think he called it the 'hijack' story. Coming out of Brussels they were hijacked by three complete loopers from N. Ireland who demanded a lift, stole their beer, and politely asked for some money for the ferry. He also talked about winning the sweep regarding how many unrelated and not so funny stories the loudest lad could tell non-stop without being interrupted. Boy did he not like to be interrupted. He was so bad that it ended up being quite funny. Total charity case vowed to avoid them for the rest of our lives."

Feeling rather sheepish and turning a light shade of red, I was rescued from my embarrassment when Edel was hailed back to the Venus flytrap.

About five minutes later I was deciding where I was heading next when I heard the sound of two full glasses hitting the table. Edel was back and her opening line was something along the lines of "I can do charity."

God only knows what happened over the next few hours though I do remember club nausea being visited. That beautiful and wonderful girl is now my wife of 24 years and we have three great kids now aged 21, 18, and 17. Sliding Doors moment again. What if I had not fallen out with Paul and Shelly Murphy?

Back in Omagh and home time. Another great day with the lads and great memories. Everything was looking rosy.

It Takes Balls…

21 Journey To National Championships

As we quickly settled on our final trip to Dublin for the National Veterans table tennis championship there was much to discuss. Firstly, there were only two of us in the car as Sean was injured and didn't want to risk it. The main topic of conversation however was coronavirus and how it might affect us all.

At 9 o clock, Paul turned on RTE for the national news. It was confirmed that there were now 19 cases in the Republic, the news also confirmed that there were 7 cases in the north. Fortunately, no deaths had been reported. I convinced Paul to turn over to BBC Radio 5 to see what was happening in the UK. The BBC reported a second death with confirmed cases rising as high as two hundred and six.

"How is this all affecting your American company, Paul?"

"Not too badly for us as a lot of our manufacturing is done overseas. There are a lot of emails and directives flying around the place. How are the stock markets holding up Des?"

"If you take the FTSE100 index as a guide, the markets are over 1200 points lower than what they had reached in mid-January. In percentage terms, that's almost a drop of 16%."

Paul asked me, "What does that mean in reality?"

"The phone calls have already started. People are concerned about their investments and pensions. With this virus thing, anything could happen over the next few months."

"Will you contact all your clients?"

I told Paul, "That is not actually possible. I will not contact them directly but I will be available for them to phone or email me. The stock market will over-sell itself because of all the stories that will turn up in the media. Then it will bounce back. The professionals will make a killing as they will start buying on all the dips."

"Can you not do that for all your clients?"

"Impossible Paul, because I do not hold discretionary powers. Instead, I invest my clients into a range of risk-targeted funds. These funds are multi-asset and are designed to protect the downside, but humans panic, and my main job in the coming months will be to stop people from doing silly things and cashing out at the bottom of the market."

Paul responded, "How do you know when the markets have bottomed?"

"With hindsight, and that is when the strange phone calls will come asking why I didn't move the client out when the markets peaked at 7,600 and rebuy when they were below 5000. However, this is what I get paid for and I have the experience of five or six major market corrections."

"No rest for the wicked then Des."

"Indeed, no rest for the wicked. Thankfully today should take my mind off everything for a couple of hours. You know I have really enjoyed all the nonsense going down to these tournaments this season," I told Paul honestly.

"We have enjoyed some of it," Paul replied speaking on behalf of himself and his sidekick Sean.

As we passed by Armagh heading to Newry my mind started drifting back to Seamus Mallon, his legacy and the responsibility that now fell on people like myself to follow through on his heroic efforts. Thankfully Seamus had lived long enough to see the SDLP fight back against Sinn Fein in the recent Westminster election of December 2019, winning three seats. Again, I was back in his house in Markethill listening to his stories about elections of old and how he loved canvassing and looking for votes during elections. The amount of abuse he would get from republicans, loyalists, and even unionists from his hometown. His stubbornness was a great asset in those moments. He would simply ignore the abuse, smile, and walk on. Stubbornness and crankiness are great characteristics if used to your advantage he once told me. I could easily identify with this.

"Have you ever thought about going into politics yourself?" Paul suddenly asked as we were driving past Markethill." He knew exactly where my mind had drifted to.

"You are not the first person to ask me that. Seamus Mallon mentioned it and a considerable number of my unionist clients have asked me over the years."

"Why is that Des?"

"Well firstly a lot of them have known me for over twenty years and realise that I do not bite. Also, my political views very much represent the middle ground. I also believe that they have recognised that a sizeable element of nationalism are no longer the enemy, or never were the enemy. However, I also discuss or have discussed their fears and I have expressed my views on their fears."

"Give me some examples Des."

"They are so fearful of a Sinn Fein dominated Republic. I

explain that a single unionist party would frequently hold the balance of power. I also show them examples of how the southern establishment is very anti-Sinn Fein and how the press will do their utmost to keep them at bay

"A second major fear is the role of the Catholic church and 'Rome rule'. I show them census results and the number of people no longer identifying as Catholics or Roman Catholics as they frequently refer to us. I always ask them when they were last in Dublin. No matter what they say I recommend a weekend or a mid-week break in Dublin. It is now a modern European multi-cultural society. I also point to the various referenda held in the south on divorce, abortion, and same-sex marriage. The Republic of Ireland is now a more secular state and unionists no longer need to fear 'Rome rule'. The conservatism of the unionist community is something that I identified with. It also helps my business that they are savers rather than spenders, unlike those Catholics/nationalists.

"Catholic only schools is another issue. I agree mainly with the unionist community on this one. I always point towards the growth of the shared/integrated education movement.

"When a client says, "Our people have suffered so much in the troubles at the hands of the IRA!" instantly I will refer them to Robert Lynch's book 'The Partition of Ireland 1918-1925'. You tend to know your history, but you need to know all of it. We have a shared history that we need to look at from different perspectives. I always float the idea of a proper peace and reconciliation forum. Let us find out about the past and use it to build a better future. I always explain why I live in Dunmullan, how much I love it, and how a shared present will build a better future.

"When they mention that "more and more Catholics/nationalists are voting Sinn Fein so they must all have supported the IRA," what role has hard unionism and loyalism played in this? is always my first response. I will tell them why I have become disaffected by recent actions of the DUP party, especially over Brexit. However, I strongly defend the DUP's right to express their views and put them to the electorate. Who is explaining soft nationalism to them and why are they not listening? When the border poll comes, they may need some support from within the soft nationalist community. They are driving that voice away completely.

"Another main issue raised is the red herring "the south couldn't afford us". Balls, balls, and more balls to that. I point out all the work being done by the likes of another Derry head Paul Gosling, an Englishman, and his work 'The Economic Effects of an All-Island Economy 2018'. Straight away I ask the question of how much we cost England. Total Blank. This is crazy stuff. Every single person living here should know this. Ask your local or national politician. The current situation can not continue as we will have to completely rebuild society after the pandemic ends. Paul, I could go on, ignorance is a very dangerous beast.

"Flags and symbols will occasionally be raised as does the role of the Orange Order and Ulster Unionist culture. I always tell them the story of cycling from Dunmullan into Newtownstewart via Gortin and Plumbridge on a blustery day. It was the only day in my life that I wanted to see a flag so I could pick the rest of my route. No bleeding flags. I also point out that I can only relate to the Irish tricolour in the south of Ireland. The republican movement has hijacked it. In our future agreed Ireland, the flag to be considered should be the four provinces flag.

"I also point out that within an agreed Ireland concept, Ulster Unionist culture will have to be promoted. I have said before that the Twelfth celebrations should be an international opportunity to the same extent as St Patrick's day is used to promote Ireland. Tolerance is one of my favourite words."

"What about Republican and Nationalist clients?" Paul asked.

"Quite a few of my nationalist clients and friends have similar views as mine. They all agree that a civic forum to discuss all issues is a great idea. To be honest with you I'm not sure how many republican clients I have. It would certainly be a tiny number, and maybe even smaller if I ever put my thoughts down on paper."

Okay, Des. One last chance to get this all off your chest. If you were put in charge what would you do? You are only allowed five main points. The political views of One Mr. Desmond Flanagan Junior, please.

22 My Vision For The Future

Firstly, whatever the people of Northern Ireland decide, we all have to work together to build on the Good Friday Agreement. We are Northern Irish and should celebrate our differences. Here are the five things that I would do to help us move forward.

1 Agreed formula for any future border poll

At present, the Secretary of State for Northern Ireland has the power to call a border poll if it appears likely that a majority would favour a united Ireland. This needs to be replaced by a set formula which, if met, triggers a border poll, say three or five years later. Why should an English minister hold this power when the people of Northern Ireland should have it? Surely Stormont could agree the set formula.

In the short term, this would probably boost unionism. All unionists would register, and it would increase participation in all future elections. Surely it would also increase the numbers of nationalists and republicans registering as well, which can only be good for constitutional politics.

A second option would be to have an indicative poll attached to all future Westminster elections. "Do you want a border poll?" A border poll could take place a set number of years later.

2 Centenary of Northern Ireland May 2021 – Academic Advisory Board

We need a non-partisan report on the history of Ireland since partition. We need an independent body to reflect back on our shared history. We need to move forward together and build a better society for everyone. But we must know what our history actually was.

3 Peace and Reconciliation Forum

I personally think that we must all tell our stories to make sure that history does not repeat itself. Let everyone come forward and tell their stories. Anybody confessing to any activity that resulted in hurt or death should either be exempt from prosecution or should receive minimum sentences.

Without understanding the past, how can we move forward? It is up to the paramilitaries and British government to confirm their participation. This may be unlikely, but the process would still be beneficial.

4 Civic Forum to be set up

A civic forum to be set up by the people for the people. Maybe this civic forum could decide on the Agreed Formula for any future border poll. Terms and conditions for the Peace and Reconciliation Forum could also be decided by this forum.

This civic forum could review the three options open to the land of many names and could ask the academic advisory board to report on them.

a) Northern Ireland staying within the United Kingdom – Status Quo

b) United Ireland

c) Agreed Ireland

We need an independent report on the viability of all three options.

5 Agreed Ireland Forum

I personally would prefer a border poll not on a United Ireland but on an Agreed Ireland. We should do the opposite of Brexit, have all the hard work done first, and then vote on the options.

Here are just a sample of things to be discussed:

A) Dual nationality to continue

Could it be extended to citizens of the Republic of

Ireland, especially unionist communities in the south?

B) Role of Stormont

C) Federal options

D) Bill of Rights

To protect all minorities.

E) Shared education

F) What educational, civil service, health service, etc to be adopted by an Agreed Ireland going forward

G) Flag/national anthem

Four provinces flag?

H) Re-join the commonwealth

As an act of good faith would the nationalist/republican communities consider this option?

A civic forum would quickly develop these initial thoughts into a proper discussion. An independent report on the benefits of all three options would be very helpful. It would then be up to the various parties to argue the merits of their preferred options.

How would the ever-increasing European and non-European population vote in both the North and the South on any future border poll? Surely they would vote on the economic benefits of either staying in the United Kingdom or entering an Agreed Ireland. This is the unknown

unknown that no politician can answer at present.

Before any border poll, we need to rebuild our society and start working together.

It Takes Balls...

23 National Championships 07/03/20

As it was the National Championships and it was also forty years since my only national title (apparently) I would be taking the over 40s much more seriously. I was drawn with Tibor Pofok and Pierre Bouhey meaning that the game with Bouhey would decide it. I duly lost to Tibor and was heading for defeat against Pierre before I launched an all-out attack. Before long I had avenged my defeat from earlier in the season. My concentration levels were good, partially due to my more settled state. There were a lot fewer things bothering me.

After Paul was knocked out at the last sixteen stage, he was soon in my corner for my match against fellow Tyrone man Rodney McKirgan, yes, 'Mr wreck my birthday' McKirgan, the man that would be playing for Ulster while I'm out losing golf balls. I was leading 2-1 in our head to head this year. This was the first year I was beating him on a head to head basis but the heavy loss at Newmills was still on my mind.

After losing the first set, coach of the year Gallagher sorted Flan the Man out and I stormed back to win 3-1 with one of my best performances of the season.

In the quarter-final, I had Rory Scott under pressure with a game point to take the game to the fifth and final set. Rory used his experience to qualify for the semi-finals where he ultimately lost.

The rest of the over 40s was highlighted by 'fast' Phil Wallace saving match points in the quarter-final against John Bowe before lifting the National Title. Well done Phil. Meanwhile many miles north, Phil's great buddy Daryl Strong was at home looking after his new daughter. Paul Gallagher reckons that his daughter will slow him down and he'll be able to sort him out next year. I am not so sure. When my children came along, I took up long-distance running to temporarily escape nappy land. Why go for a five-mile run when you can go for a fifteen-mile run?

My over 50s group was dangerous, but I was highly focused. Norman Nabney, Dave Gibbons, and Dangerous Dave Pender. First up Norman Nabney, non-playing captain to the over 40s interpro team, the man that played Paul Gallagher but not me a few years earlier. The man that I had fallen out with until I asked myself a simple question. If you had been Norman Nabney Des, would you have played Desmond Flanagan? When I answered no, I stopped falling out with Norman.

9-1 Down to Norman was never part of my plan. Beating him 12-10 was a great response and a few minutes later a 3-0 win was achieved. Doubly great in case of the dreaded countback. 3-1 victory over dangerous Dave and the same scoreline against Dave Gibbons meant I was one game away from an international comeback.

When I was called to play my Big Willie Cherry I was surprised that it was a quarter-final. I was so surprised that I was soon 2 sets down. Then it dawned in me. I had won my group and because of numbers got straight through to the quarter-finals. I noticed Phil Shaw playing Dave Gibbons on the table beside me. I was confused.com. If Phil won, I was an international player again.

Just at the end of my second set I saw that Phil had beaten Mr Gibbons. My season long goal had been achieved. But what about going for the double? International table tennis and National champion. My Big Willie was in the way. The entire third set I hung on and hung on and somehow won it. Same in the fourth and somehow I got to deuce in the set. Win this one and I would get him in the decider. Unfortunately, this is not the movies so I did not become national champion. Willie was surprised when I called him Big Willie but sat down happy. I had fought like hell but lost trying my best, and I was an international table tennis player again. After forty years I would be able to torture my son Keelan with this particular piece of information.

What about my hero Paul playing the smaller of the big two? He had beaten Kevin Mackey in two recent non-vets tournaments and was slowly torturing him to death with his high-intensity blocking game, unleashing the famous Donegal slap occasionally. 3-1 victory and next up was 'The Octopus,' Mark McAlister.

This was a curious game. Whoever won this game would be reserve in the Ireland A team rather than number one on the B team. Mark won 3-1 and when quizzed, Paul's legal team advised him to say the following "Mark's a good player and sure the prize for losing is getting to play international table tennis with Des Flanagan, enough said."

In the final I wanted Mark to beat Pat McCloughan but in a very strange game, Mark nearly forced the game into a deciding fifth set. However, Pat won and deservedly took another national title.

However, the fun was not yet over. The season started in New York with Brian F..king Finn and the now newly named Brian Finn was playing the legendary Tommy Caffery in the final of the Irish over 60s championship. Myself, Paul, and eventually the entire hall watched as Mr. Finn put in a masterful tactical game against the legend. He hung on and battled like hell, finally achieving his first national title. The joy on his face was incredible. It was the happiest I had ever seen him or anybody else after winning a stupid table tennis game. Brian Finn, one of the most popular people in Irish table tennis, I salute you. No better way to end a season. See you all in Dublin for the Six Nations was what I was thinking as we headed for the car and the journey home.

Final Rankings for the Over 50s

<u>Ireland A-Team</u>

1 -Pat McCloughan

2 -Kevin Mackey

3 -Mark McAlister

<u>Ireland B Team</u>

4 -Paul Gallagher

5 -Des Flanagan

6 -Philip Shaw

24 Journey Home From National Championships

"So Des, after a full year of this we end up on the same team," stated a delighted Paul.

"How does the competition actually work? How many games per match and what about the doubles?" I asked.

"You play two singles and one doubles, so five matches in total against all the other home nations."

I asked Paul, "So who picks the players for each game?"

"I will because I will be the number one ranked player," said Paul.

"No harm Paul, but to stop troubles breaking out it will be safer if I just assume the captaincy and sort out the team. Maybe best that the non singles player plays in the doubles so everyone gets a match."

"Des, I will be the captain and you can be my number two," Paul responded.

I replied, "Des Flanagan and the number two are things that don't go together."

"Awful pity we didn't get Sean into the team as well.

Could you imagine the northwest bus being the entire team with me as captain?" stated Paul.

"Sounds great but only with me as captain," I replied

"The three of us could vote on it."

"No chance, you two clowns would stitch me up."

The nonsense continued until we got to the Applegreen.

Paul announced, "As captain of the Ireland B team, I nominate Desmond Flanagan as the purchaser of coffees and Magnums."

I countered, "As the future captain of the Ireland B team, I offer to buy the coffees and magnums as a gesture of good will."

As Paul was slowly dismantling yet another Magnum ice cream sponsored by Des Flanagan Investment Solutions of James Street Omagh, he threw another curve ball at me.

"If we transfer Mark McAlister out of the A-team into my team we would be able to train together in the north west and appoint Sean McAnaney as our head coach. We would also be able to have team bonding meetings and, if you behave yourself, we might let you play in one of the smaller matches."

I responded, "I thought you said you have not had a single drink in eight years. You are talking like a drunk man. However, I think we would make a great team. Mark and I will beat the English at the doubles. Just think the octopus and me on the same side. I could wind him up from the same side of the table. This is a fantastic idea."

Paul said, "We will play a massive double round-robin the weekend before the home internationals and that will decide the playing order."

We both started laughing and congratulating ourselves on the idea and also on yet another great year playing table tennis.

"Can I tell Mark what is happening?" I pleaded.

"You do realise that he will jump at it, but he will also want to be captain."

"Three captains in one team, how will that work?" More laughter ensued.

This was the level of conversation most of the way home. After nodding to Seamus Mallon when we passed Markethill, I turned the tables on Paul.

"Paul let's say you are now in sole charge of table tennis Ireland, how would you sort it out?"

Quick as a flash and quicker than he had moved all season, he was off with idea after idea. "We need to organise twenty tournaments a year throughout the country. Table Tennis Ireland to pay the clubs to organise the tournaments, with any sponsorship raised by the clubs to go towards prizes and the clubs themselves. Greater promotion of vets table tennis as these people are in a better position to start new clubs thus promoting junior table tennis. Organise four provincial centres of excellence, with four regional hubs for the level below. Get an ideas forum up and running. See if it would be possible to get some full-time clubs established. Also, we need to completely revamp that Table Tennis Ireland website."

For the next twenty minutes, there was no stopping the Donegal Slapper. If Sean had been in the car we would probably have had to pull over with me being dispatched to get further coffees and Magnums. It was great to listen to a good friend enthusiastically fire off idea after idea.

Despite all the new Coronavirus rules we finished the season with a big hug and an even bigger laugh as we headed off home in different directions. Paul back to Letterkenny to Helen, John, and his beloved Leo, and myself back to Edel, Anna, Keelan, and Cormac. We are both very lucky lads.

25 2051

Arlene Foster is now Taoiseach in a minority government with Fine Gael. Arlene had refused to go into partnership with 'the greens'. I have been promoted to the position of Minister of Sport (better to have that clown inside causing trouble then outside wrecking the place) having stood as Fine Gael's first candidate in the north after the runaway success of my first novel.

Arlene Foster has kindly asked me to address her first cabinet after the first elections in a new agreed Ireland (even though only 50.05% had actually agreed). I start by stating that Casement Park in West Belfast will shortly open after a series of delays. I also announce that the All Ireland Club Finals will be played at Casement Park on our new national day 17th of July 2051. This date had been agreed with the support of the new Minister for Education Anthony White (the most intelligent member of the cabinet from Omagh.)

The selection of the 17th of July has been Mr. Flanagan's highlight in his short but colourful cabinet career.

"We will take the 17th part from St Paddy's day and you lot can have the July part, simply because it is warmer in July than in March."

Mr. Flanagan was currently trying to organise the order of the various orange and green marching bands and had decided on alternating bands. Orange band followed by green bands just to keep everyone happy but in reality, simply annoying everyone.

The second and final scandal had just hit Mr. Flanagan within three months of his first cabinet position. The strange payment of £127,121 via an account in the name of Sean McAnaney for the formation of two new junior football teams in the north west. Namely Londonderry Celtic FC and Derry Rangers FC. Both formed to act as feeder clubs to Omagh Town FC (reformed with a kind donation from Desmond Flanagan).

18th July 2052

Political career now well and truly over due to one further financial scandal, Des is sitting in the plush offices of Des Flanagan Investment Solutions, still the only financial services company on James Street, now run by Junior. Des is staring blankly at a massive framed photograph on his wall. As usual, he had opted for an understatement caption below the frame.

"Des defends his over 80s National title against Mark 'the octopus' McAlister."

The previous year he had defeated a rather frail Brian Finn in the final after controversially sacking his coach Paul Gallagher for the world record 179th time. Shining out from the photograph and hard to miss was his big Willie. Mr. Willie Cherry had been given a substantial sports grant to become Desmond Flanagan's latest coach.

"Des, Des wake up for God's sake. Are you dreaming or having nightmares?"

"Dreaming I believe. What date is it Edel?"

"Edel responded "It's the 30th of May. Here is your

phone, it has been ringing all morning."

"Okay, okay" I responded. "One final question. "What year is it and any chance of a cup of tea?"

"2020 you fool and no." With that Edel was off and I was totally confused.

On the screen of my phone were two numbers. Derry head McAnaney and the Donegal Slapper. Trying to clear my head I phoned Paul first. "Are we training today?"

He said, "No, did you get that email this morning?"

"What email and what the hell is going on?"

"It is cancelled," he announced. "Due to the coronavirus."

"What is cancelled?" I asked, getting slightly frustrated.

"The Home Nations Championship in Dublin."

Suddenly wide awake I ask again, "What?"

"Its over, me, you, and Mark will not be playing for the Ireland B team."

"Does this mean I'm still an international table tennis player?" I pleaded.

"How can you be classed as an international table tennis player if you have not played international table tennis, you clown?"

Balls, balls, and more balls. We quickly ended the phone call.

"Does this mean I have to do this all over again next year?" I thought out loud, before diving back under the duvet with a particularly stupid grin on my face.

About The Author

Des is one of the most dedicated people I have ever met, dedicated to his family, dedicated to others, and dedicated to the future. Through this whole process of writing this book, he has had great patience dealing with me and any other hiccups that came up along the way. He has worked as a financial advisor since November 1992 and because of his relationship with his client base has become very interested in how we build a shared future going forward.

-Cormac Flanagan-

Printed in Great Britain
by Amazon

19180919R00113